THE
METAVERSE
WORKPLACE
REVOLUTION

A Path to Greater Profitability,
a Stronger Culture, and Industry Disruption

THE
METAVERSE
WORKPLACE
REVOLUTION

JASON GESING

FAST
COMPANY
Press

Image courtesy of Virbela

Fast Company Press
New York, New York
www.fastcompanypress.com

Distributed by Greenleaf Book Group

For ordering information or special discounts for bulk purchases, please contact Greenleaf Book Group at PO Box 91869, Austin, TX 78709, 512.891.6100.

Design and composition by Greenleaf Book Group and Mimi Bark
Cover design by Greenleaf Book Group and Mimi Bark

Publisher's Cataloging-in-Publication data is available.

Print ISBN: 978-1-63908-080-9

eBook ISBN: 978-1-63908-081-6

To offset the number of trees consumed in the printing of our books, Greenleaf donates a portion of the proceeds from each printing to the Arbor Day Foundation. Greenleaf Book Group has replaced over 50,000 trees since 2007.

Printed in the United States of America on acid-free paper

24 25 26 27 28 29 30 31   10 9 8 7 6 5 4 3 2 1

First Edition

CONTENTS

FOREWORD

WHILE MANY PONTIFICATE about the endless possibilities of working in the Metaverse, Jason Gesing has already erected a multibillion-dollar enterprise within it. In a world awash with theorists, he stands alone as a practitioner, having brought to life what most merely sketch on whiteboards. If there's one person on this planet supremely qualified to pen a manual on the Metaverse workplace revolution, it's Jason. His journey, from concept to colossal success, isn't just noteworthy—it's unparalleled.

Having witnessed him grow an organization from 1,000 to 86,000-plus people, I can confirm it is not his technological prowess that has led to his success but rather his understanding and sense of value of the people he leads. As an organizational psychologist and a founder of the enterprise Metaverse platform that Jason has built upon, I can testify that it is the understanding of people—as individuals, teams, and communities—that differentiates a successful versus unsuccessful implementation of the Metaverse.

The Metaverse Workplace Revolution is not just a handbook for business leaders looking to navigate this brave new world, it's a philosophical exploration of what work can and should be. By addressing crucial focal points, from productivity to corporate well-being, Jason presents a holistic vision for the future workplace. A place where spatial computing meets human connectivity, where boundaries are expanded yet inclusivity reigns supreme.

Following a COVID-driven shakeout and global remote working revolution, many companies are still struggling to redefine what a new era of work means to them. As we stand at this crossroad, the decisions business leaders make will have repercussions for decades to come. The freedom of remote working practices only touches the surface. The Metaverse will bring opportunities we are not even capable of imagining today, but hesitation before the unknown and an unclear path remains. Having someone that's charting that path today creates an invaluable guide for those who seek to not only survive but thrive in this digital renaissance. It's an encouraging call to be part of the revolution and to embrace the vast horizons of possibility the Metaverse offers.

As you dive into the pages that follow, let yourself be challenged, inspired, and enlightened. The future of work is not just about new technologies—it's about a mindset, a vision, and the courage to redefine what's possible. Let *The Metaverse Workplace Revolution* be your compass as we journey together into this uncharted territory.

—Alex Howland, PhD,
Co-founder and president of Virbela
September 4, 2023

INTRODUCTION

IF YOU JOIN me for a tour of the OMNUS Metaverse campus (the "Omnusverse"), you'll be invited to create a life-like avatar of yourself—complete with distinctive facial features, hairstyles, and clothing. Two lines of text appear over your avatar's head, noting your name and your role or region. Once you've designed your virtual body, you are given access to a virtual island surrounded by a protective digital "hedge" that presents visually as a body of water. Now you can freely roam the cyberterrain.

Our starting point is the "heart" of OMNUS: the main auditorium, where larger meetings with attendees from anywhere around the world can take place. Positioned in the center of the island, the Community Center is one of the biggest buildings within the digital landscape. Once inside, your avatar can choose from available seats in an expansive auditorium. Because presentations draw hundreds of people, the space offers four levels of seating that are separated into three large sections. All of the seats face a wide stage, which is covered with decorative flags.

Overhead, colorful can lights shine over parted curtains. The primary focus of this space consists of three presentation screens designed for video displays and slideshow demonstrations.

Lining the walls are extra doors for an easy exit after community gatherings. (Even avatars rush the doors.) The building is surrounded by grassy knolls, waterfalls, and paved areas for seating. Even more interesting are the amenities positioned throughout the island. You will see virtual sports spaces, areas for lounging along the beach, a speedboat dock with stationed crafts for quick trips around the island, and—most entertaining of all—a pirate ship, for both exploration and additional meeting space.

Amid these virtual structures stand two tall towers that serve as OMNUS's headquarters. Each floor can be designated to individual countries, regions, and states. For example, if you are curious about a matter in North Carolina, we can take the elevator to that region's floor and observe their open concept office design—complete with vaulted ceilings, tall windows, sprawling tables, barstools, and cozy lounge spaces to accommodate large groups. Private offices and meeting rooms line the space, as do plants, paintings, and additional presentation screens.

You may want to drop by the Information Desk to find everything from maps of this virtual world and materials on the company, to safety guidelines on the Metaverse at large. As we move through the campus, we will encounter other avatars—both human and artificial intelligence (AI) bots—that will show you how "organic" Metaverse interactions can be.

Until you experience an interactive virtual reality, you can hardly grasp the fluidity of our melding worlds. Everything that is possible in the real world is possible in the Metaverse—from experiencing the energetic boost after a motivational presentation to the nagging inconveniences of everyday living. Yes, you may bump into coworkers—literally; you may trip down the stairs and spill your virtual coffee; in some virtual landscapes, avatars can even experience the dreaded "awkward door hold."

What I am describing here is the Metaverse workplace. It is a cousin to the Metaverse world of gaming, but it serves a very different purpose.

The term "Metaverse" seems to be a catch-all term for anything video and online related. Is it a video game, a virtual realm, or just a clunky version of Zoom? Opinions differ, and the definition of this concept remains elusive. But think of the Metaverse less as a type of technology or even an application of it, than as a new way of interacting in the digital space. You might put on a virtual reality (VR) headset or augmented reality glasses to do so—or you might simply use your laptop with an internet connection to jump into your organization's Metaverse as an avatar.

To put it another way, a Metaverse workplace is a persistent virtual world: always there, in the same way your physical office space is. It is the primary place where a company accommodates its employees, holds meetings, trains new hires, provides everything from a coffee machine to a pool table, and in general does business. And the way you turn up there is in your avatar form.

Right now, you might be thinking, "Well, isn't that what online games like Fortnite do?" True, but to say that Fortnite is the Metaverse is a little like saying that Google is the internet.

In a work sense, a professional Metaverse platform empowers

corporations, professionals, educational organizations, and event organizers to create their own virtual worlds, offer services to their clients, and facilitate engagement among employees, customers, and suppliers in a business-focused environment. I have been working in the Metaverse for more than a dozen years now. And I have seen how fruitful it has been, is, and can be in the future for professional services firms and the professionals within them—whether real estate brokerages, law firms, or other service-based businesses—really, any organization for whom social interaction, communication, and scalability are priorities.

The notion that the Metaverse is a scary place is untrue—but it *is* a disruptive place. My goal is that it disrupts Western work culture for the better so that we can be spurred into a more innovative and values-driven professional landscape. In this book, I set out to show you that a Metaverse workplace is not only a possibility, but the most effective way of applying a Metaverse work model to service industry organizations. I draw on over a decade of metaverse experience to address twelve "tensions" that should be at the front of any business leader's mind as they consider applying a Metaverse work model: from productivity and profitability to social equality and corporate well-being.

I am not alone in predicting that in the next two decades, the world at large will be transitioning to the Metaverse. Business owners who understand, embrace, and prepare for the best (and the worst) of its possibilities will be on the cutting edge of technology, with a competitive advantage, set to lead in their respective industries. While the tensions within any transition are inevitable, I learned early on that all things virtual can amplify the values that operate them.

When you finish reading this book—whether you start at the beginning and read through to the end, or dive into the chapters that intrigue you the most—I hope you will come to share with me a vision for building a unified organizational culture that can dominate in its industry, while at the same time valuing its people.

Image courtesy of Virbela

1

WHERE PIVOTING MEETS PROFIT

My Introduction to the Metaverse — The Case Study of eXp

I first became an avatar in January of 2010.

After going to law school and joining a law firm to begin what I hoped would be a rewarding and fulfilling career as an attorney, I learned that in Massachusetts, an attorney can easily obtain their managing real estate broker credential. Meaning, not only could I have any professional advantages of being both a practicing attorney and a broker in the state where I lived, but I would also be able to engage in transactions if I wished to, or ultimately could grow and oversee a team of agents. The idea of being able to lead according to my own ways of thinking excited me.

When a colleague introduced me to Glenn Sanford, I had no idea that he'd be ushering me into an entirely new universe (quite literally). Glenn had been running what was effectively a traditional brokerage but utilizing online leads. This was something still relatively new at the time: the idea that you could generate business via the internet. Then, in October 2009, Glenn launched a company called eXp Realty. In December 2009, an acquaintance introduced me to Glenn for the very first time, and I knew I wanted to be involved in eXp.

We literally met in the Metaverse.

"Would you like to become an avatar?" Glenn offered. He sent me a link to join eXp's Metaverse campus, where I could see humanlike animations traversing—and bouncing off each other—across the computer screen. It seemed gimmicky at first, but as I became more comfortable with the technology, it piqued my interest.

Little did I know how integral a couple thousand pixels on a screen would be to the following years of my life. "This is going to change the future of real estate," Glenn assured me—a radical proposition to a tech neophyte like me.

For six months we worked together as avatars before we ever met in person; in reality, we lived three thousand miles apart—Glenn in Washington state and I in Massachusetts. So began my path of growing and working for eXp Realty in the Metaverse as part of the small, organic "leadership team" we had at the time. My desire was to escape law, and I tried long and hard to find an alternative career that would enable me to utilize my law degree. The quest was harder than expected and, in order to try and preserve my sanity by introducing some variety to my work, I began to dabble in real estate—a field that would meld the seemingly random facets of my working life up to that point into a comprehensive representation of my business values. Yet the Metaverse introduced me to something even larger: the possibility of a work environment that could apply to all service-based companies, enabling them to connect and expand in a way that surpassed all expectations.

I'd been taught there was one way of engaging the customer: building in-person connections and being physically present for every meeting, every work function, every casual interaction with one's colleagues. The idea of technologizing relationships seemed to break the rules of engagement (and also seemed a little far-fetched) because digital community liaisons—including the use of social media websites—had only been popular for about a decade.

Plus, back then, everything was much less definitive and well-formed. This platform eXp was using wasn't called the Metaverse; they didn't even have a name for it. Computers were still in their clunky "dinosaur" form, and the technology was rudimentary compared to the high-definition avatars and campus settings we have today. Given the standard functions of the internet in the early 2000s, it was hard to conceptualize the benefits of a remote workspace stacked against the established real estate model.

After all, the original way of doing things represented stability. It was a proven way of operating a business, supplemented by a conventional prototype of community building. What the traditional model lacked was modernized ideas, virtual scalability, environmental sustainability, long-term profitability, and innovative approaches to solving old problems—a combination of my (emerging) professional values. To embrace something so progressive seemed like a major risk at the time.

On the computer screen, my digital avatar consisted of one large block for my physical body, and a smaller block for my head featuring a one-dimensional picture of my face. The running joke was that you'd have to be a blockhead to consider it.

Though it was a far cry from what the Metaverse would become—a space where three-dimensional (3-D) simulations of everyone in our organization can roam beaches together, build virtual campfires, take treks in the woods, or visit the digital boardrooms of any campus—it was still ahead of its time. Sure, there were no locations and no spawning points, making it difficult to coordinate two avatars in the same virtual plane, but the fact that I could exist in a world that was not my own meant huge possibilities for a potentially global work environment. And just so you know, my present-day avatar is far more detailed, much more humanlike, and includes details that truly represent my physical self when it comes to hair, eye color, skin tone, and even accessories.

I could see the scalability potential in those strange, multi-colored avatars awkwardly bumping into each other. I began to consider the profitability of abandoning the traditional way of doing business, even if it meant leaning into the most bizarre idea I'd ever seen. Bear in mind, it was 2010—the iPhone was still in its genesis, and I was still committed to my BlackBerry. But I found myself believing this was the way of the future. I was sure that if we could do this well, that it could be very profitable indeed.

Image courtesy of Virbela

One thing I knew for sure was that I had no interest in standing still. My professional landscape, up to that point, had been relatively bleak. I'd seen the downside of the conventional work model at my previous law firm: logging more hours than I could count, trying to pay mounting bills, sitting stuck in peak-hour traffic, and never getting to see my kids.

To top it off, no one ever stepped foot in our law offices. If we were required to meet with a client for mediation or negotiation, it was always off-site. Still, lawyers were spending exorbitant amounts of money in fixed costs that weren't about utility. This was the logic of the traditional world I worked in. Then there was eXp, whose business model was built almost entirely on recognizing that offices' utility had been diminished and that costs associated with physical offices and redundant staffing inevitably were funded by the service professionals who were part of the industry—by giving up a greater percentage of their commissions or paying more fees. Perhaps service professionals had always been aware that clients were paying for these amenities, but not that they themselves were also being charged.

eXp's success, however, was far from immediate.

"Aren't you guys cute!" passersby would say as they surveyed our booth at real estate industry trade shows. There, I would be promoting our virtual brokerage, touting our resourcefulness, excellent compensation model, and low fee structure.

People weren't buying it. It didn't matter that eXp had created a sustainable formula to make the company indestructible during financial fallout. It didn't matter that they had relieved themselves of office and infrastructure costs. These radical solutions initially fell on deaf ears. This didn't surprise me, because—for the most part—people have to be in desperate positions before they will consider a new way of doing things. Especially if those new ways are ahead of their time. In 2010, most of us were decidedly risk averse. The global financial crisis of 2008 caused havoc in the real estate market and hardship for many property owners. I was one of them: I'd been seriously burned on an investment in a Boston apartment building, leaving me in a tenuous financial position. When I left my law job in early 2010, I launched my own solo law practice and also joined eXp.

Early on with eXp I was making $500 per month at best, and my law practice neither interested me nor succeeded. My wife, who is also an attorney, was caring for our two children (aged three and one at the time), and we had no health coverage. We found ourselves one day sitting in front of a caseworker pleading for public assistance so we could continue to pay our bills. It was the most humbling moment of my life. We were denied assistance because we owned two cars . . . one of which was a bright red, 2003 Hyundai Santa Fe with no functioning door handle on the driver's side and a transmission that wouldn't move beyond second gear whenever it rained outside, prompting back-road travel rather than interstate even if it took exponentially longer to arrive at a destination.

I share all this because this sobering reality and my desperation made eXp's success, and my own success within it, an all-or-nothing proposition. eXp absolutely had to work or I was going to be in my forties with no real income, no career path, and even less opportunity. Fortunately, we persevered, and my wife, to her tremendous credit, never once failed to support me in my pursuit of making eXp a tremendous success and, ultimately, the single largest brokerage in the residential real estate industry.

Our competitors couldn't understand that one of our major areas of profitability had come from our successful effort to expand to various geographical locations. In the traditional real estate model, getting agents to join you if they lived more than fifteen or twenty miles away from your office building was almost impossible. To make matters worse, licensing in one state had zero value for brokers looking to practice in other states unless they had additional licenses and a physical meeting space. Traditional models carried a tremendous risk of expanding outside their geographical location, ultimately limiting scalability or collapsing businesses entirely.

These geographical issues became evident as we began speaking with other brokerage owners who were itching to sell their small businesses due to a lack of deals and profitability across the board in the midst of a global financial crisis.

Finally, my law degree would benefit me. I became familiar with state licensing regulations, brainstorming various paths forward. Once I arrived at a chosen path in a market, eXp was able to commence operations in that market and ultimately pursue opportunities across the United States. The company became more stable and recognizable—until within a small number of years it became the go-to industry source. The beauty was that eXp had liberties other companies didn't, because they had cut costs early and reallocated money in the right places, including, most notably, agent compensation.

Soon, eXp became a threatening competitor to the larger, global real estate brands, nearly all of which were operating under a franchise structure, resulting in independently owned offices in locations where the demographics supported franchisee investment and launch. Those agents who were located in more rural areas or those isolated by natural boundaries, such as mountain ranges, often were forced to choose among a handful of small independent brokerages with compensation models that were far inferior to what even the franchise brands were offering, notwithstanding their brick-and-mortar–intensive approach. Because it didn't make sense for franchises to invest in these more sparsely populated areas, the opportunities that existed within them were limited at best. Meanwhile, it was inexpensive and profitable all around for eXp to expand geographically but fully virtually. Today, eXp has gained ground and a solid name, and is able to approach markets other agencies wouldn't consider. This means large real estate franchises no longer laugh at the little guy—because eXp is a real estate Goliath.

Throughout the following decade, eXp Realty would expand

throughout more than twenty countries, employing more than eighty thousand agents and becoming the largest operating subsidiary of eXp World Holdings, Inc., a NASDAQ-listed company. In time, eXp Realty would become the fastest growing residential real estate brokerage in the history of the industry in North America—and arguably, the world.

While I am no longer involved with the eXp team on a daily basis, my experiences there have shaped my journey in co-founding OMNUS. At OMNUS, we are working to transform and improve the lives of attorneys by illustrating the cost effectiveness and dominant competitive advantages that can be unlocked with Metaverse technologies, and we do so through use of a Metaverse workplace model ourselves.

I would go on to live out those early predictions about the Metaverse as an avatar: exploring the infinite virtual space where pivoting generates profit, grateful that, while standing on the precipice of a technological revolution, I chose the unconventional option—to leap.

Pivot to Lead

In March 2020, the coronavirus pandemic hit full force, closing offices indefinitely across the nation, and the real estate industry was no exception. Agents packed their belongings, prohibited from practicing at their workplaces or doing showings of any kind. State regulators closed recording offices, making transactions impossible to process. Residential real estate agents were apprehensive that transactions would come to a grinding halt and that the market would stagnate and decline until a vaccine became available. When the opposite happened, experts in the industry were surprised.

Due to historically low interest rates and the ability of employees to work from wherever they wanted, March 2020 to February 2022 proved to be one of the most robust housing markets in modern history. Traditional second-home markets became primary markets. Families priced out of large cities could purchase more space at a lesser cost in outlying areas.

As a result, families were reconnected, work-life balance improved, and employee satisfaction increased.

Then the end of February 2022 came, and the market slowed due to a rise in interest rates precipitated by soaring inflation. Within seven months, the market was stagnant and most brokerages experienced double-digit declines year over year in both transaction count and revenue.

In the midst of this, the fixed costs associated with traditional brick-and-mortar businesses didn't change: office rents, staffing the same functions in multiple locations, common area maintenance charges, telecommunication systems, photocopier maintenance, and more. These hard costs remained in place, leaving those without a plan unable to generate a steady profit.

Those still in the grips of a franchise structure or caught off guard by global changes were flat-footed in maintaining lucrativeness, sustainability, an effective operations process, connectivity, and company culture. **They had no idea how to operate virtually—because they'd never considered it.**

And this lack of foresight cost them. A 2022 earnings report of all major publicly traded United States brokerages demonstrated widespread losses. Though these losses were expected and acceptable while the market was thriving, they were crippling businesses that would have otherwise excelled if they'd embraced a virtual culture.

In looking at how organizations generally responded to the pandemic, eXp is a case study in innovation and in being structured with minimal fixed costs, which allowed the company to pivot and quickly adjust costs upward or downward depending on market conditions. Amid international panic and economic downturn, eXp thrived above the rest, with profitable numbers for many consecutive quarters. They demonstrated a lower cost per transaction while expanding geographically. eXp was ready when the call to "go remote" sounded. They'd already pivoted years prior, becoming pioneers in the digital space. When the stay-at-home mandates came, there was no scrambling to establish work-from-home policies and procedures. No scurrying to gather, pack up, ship, and lend expensive laptops, headphone sets, computer cameras, or technological supplies to individual workers. No extensive employee release-and-return strategies. No need for masks, hand sanitizer, or printing multiple copies of laminated World Health Organization protocols. No fear about the impact of global crisis on company culture.

There was no reason to panic. In fact, employees were grateful for the remote structure that had been solidified since the company came into existence in 2009.

So, what was the secret to eXp's success? Well, it all began with learning from the mistakes of other organizations. And taking notes throughout a previous financial crisis, the market crash of 2007 that fueled its decision to go fully remote, recognizing that if they didn't overhaul their cost structure dramatically, they wouldn't survive the next market crash—nor would they thrive in the interim.

eXp's leadership team, effectively from day 1, opened their minds and laptops to virtual liaisons, establishing processes for our Cloud work environment. They were inspired early on by the idea of a metaverse campus approach, complete with digital avatars: humanlike representations of themselves across markets far and wide. These avatars could host meetings, play games, chat, connect, and do what everyone at eXp was there to do—sell real estate.

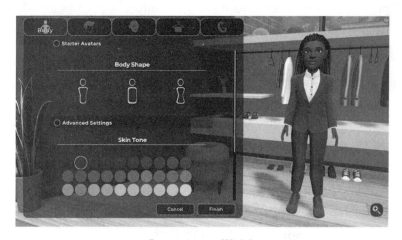

Image courtesy of Virbela

Through the use of the Metaverse, eXp could process transactions, train support staff, and nurture new agents at a fraction of the cost of its competitors, all in a profitable and sustainable business model, and with a commitment to avoid brick-and-mortar costs and redundant staffing expenses.

With more than a decade of digital traction, 2020 through 2022 were the most lucrative years in eXp's history. In 2021, revenue increased by 110 percent. Net income soared over 162 percent. The organization's net promoter score (the gold standard in depicting customer satisfaction) was 71/100, a rarely attained achievement. In Glassdoor's 2021 ratings, eXp was ranked fourth overall among large companies. And to top it all off—by 2022, eXp had declared their third dividend.

These metrics indicate eXp's early ability to pivot for profit and maintain an effectual model where people enjoy working and doing business—even in the midst of global panic.

I use eXp here as a case study because I have seen in real time how a Metaverse-based business model can succeed. That is why I urge leaders in the service sector to take initiative. When considering profitability, it's not just about the next six months; it's about the next decade. I've spent the past year intentionally considering where service industries would fall in a significant downturn. This is not because I am a pessimist; it's because I am confident a downturn is on the horizon and is likely to last several years.

When I consider profitability for OMNUS over the next year and a half, staying in business and keeping the greatest number of people employed are my two fundamental goals. I firmly believe that the preparations and precautions an organization takes now will make it a leader in its respective industry twelve to twenty-four months down the line. Inevitably, those who have clung to their high-rise offices, break rooms, and cubicle spaces will close their doors—or look to a new model and find doors opening in abundance. The Metaverse model offers a value proposition to the service sector at large: transform and grow; don't get left behind. The Metaverse has space for you.

Even amid an abundant market, I see many companies in the service sector that haven't proven profitable. They've accumulated mountains of debt and have shown no ability to generate positive earnings before interest and taxes or earnings of any kind—and those issues will likely grow only more pronounced in a crisis. As economic activity slows, the traditional way of doing business will create a bottleneck—resulting in a negative financial impact that will inevitably detract top talent.

Top talent individuals have high standards; they don't underestimate the value of their time and resources. This is especially true for millennial and Gen Z professionals, who want to feel ideologically aligned with their places of work. More than ever, employees in the Western world want to work for sophisticated remote organizations—founded upon solid principles that do not operate with unnecessary costs. They are drawn to meaningful, accessible work that can be done cost-effectively from a home office. They understand that professional goals can be met outside the boardroom. Companies that are quick to recognize this and appeal to these professionals will remain competitive in their industries.

One such leader is Hewlett Packard Enterprise (HPE), an organization that is shifting its work model to appeal to future generations. Workplace expert Jennifer Moss writes, "To address this very real issue of attraction, retention, [and] solid attrition, HPE conducted an internal survey and found that almost two-thirds of its workforce wanted to spend only 20 percent or less time working at a shared physical site."[1] She quotes Alan May, chief people officer at HPE: "We know that when team members feel that they have balance, they are more productive and more likely to build a career [here]. The pandemic caused people to re-evaluate what was important to them." May's remark is a sentiment many companies are coming to recognize as they prepare to shift in response.

This is a call to all business owners to evaluate their purpose and resources. Now is an excellent time to establish long-term tenets and sustainable goals. This should include an evaluation of physical assets and brick-and-mortar establishments. If the property is not serving the business, it's time to let it go.

I'll give a pass to those selling physical goods. If yours is a business where items or perishables are best sold off a shelf, or in-person appointments are necessary (a restaurant, a barber shop, a physical therapist)—it makes sense to have physical space. But if you're an accountant, a lawyer, or a graphic designer; or the business is a call center, a collection agency, or an insurance agency—why accrue unnecessary business expenses? Why not bank the extra money and insulate the company in difficult times? Or why not invest in growth by offering more attractive compensation to the professionals in your employ than any of your competitors?

Take insurance agents as an example. Assume that the average home and auto policy is around $3,000 per year. The salesperson who generates the business might earn $200 for the sale (mainly due to middle management who occupy offices, even though they don't *need* that expense). Imagine how much revenue could be generated for everyone involved by cutting the costs of boardrooms they don't utilize, chairs for clients who never visit, and break rooms with rarely used refrigerators. The

Metaverse has a model that is much better for you, your employees, and your financial goals.

Almost every service-sector organization would benefit from considering a virtual model, whether they are focused solely on the monetary bottom line or have the vision to scale globally, cultivate community, or secure sustainability through economic pitfalls. I use eXp as a case study to inspire leaders who want to spend their money in the right places because I understand the future is *here* and the future is *fast*—after all, eXp has been living in the future for over thirteen years now.

With zero secured office space and zero compromises on the quality of its staff or agent support, eXp has become a global influencer because they decided to pivot early—and other businesses should, too. Pivot to profit, pivot to innovate, pivot to sustain, and pivot to lead.

Moving Meta—on Purpose

In a post-pandemic era, it surprises me that so many business leaders are unaware of or still question the profitable, versatile offerings of the Metaverse. Especially since we've seen most Western organizations spend at least one year trying to navigate parallel hybrid models using costly equipment and ineffective technologies. Meanwhile, Metaverse-based organizations were far less impacted by the pandemic—many demonstrated a track record of thriving financially and culturally despite the downturn of the economy.

If there's anything I can impress upon business leaders, it's to pay attention to new ideas, no matter how outlandish they seem. Often, innovative concepts sound unusual because conventional organizations are out of touch with industry trends. Great thought leaders on the precipice of something genius typically come off as "odd" because they are thinking ahead and moving in a particular direction *on purpose*. The same can be said about forward-thinking brands that are publicly snubbed before making their mark.

Take Netflix, for example. Consumers found their business model bizarre when they first came on the scene in 1997 with DVDs that could be ordered through the mail. The service seemed absurd because the public hadn't fully transitioned from using VHS tapes. Their primary competitor and rental industry giant, Blockbuster, had brick-and-mortar locations throughout the US. Little did Blockbuster anticipate the potential of DVDs for home use, digital movies for cinema distributors, and, eventually, today's streaming services.

The forethought of Netflix that made them seem audacious in the beginning was the catalyst to Blockbuster's downfall and eventual filing for bankruptcy—all within the span of a decade. In 2020 (the year of international streaming), the value of Netflix grew to more than two hundred billion dollars, marking a 4,060 percent increase since its transition to a streaming service in 2008 and its takedown of Blockbuster in 2010.[2] Who are the blockheads now?

Some business owners cannot yet conceptualize the trajectory of global, digital commerce. Now is the time to take notes from thought leaders and tech giants, interpret international trends, go virtual, and create sustainable business models.

Where once we pivoted only because of the pandemic, now we pivot on purpose.

Now is the time to make the choice: adapt or collapse.

Alexander Fernandez is co-founder and chief executive officer (CEO) of Streamline Media Group, a video game and Metaverse development company. Writing in *Forbes* on the Metaverse and the future of work, he references "creative destruction," an economic theory that explains how innovation enables visionary companies to replace their stagnant counterparts that resist technological progress. He states that between rapid digital advances and the economic disruption caused by COVID-19, the only way to survive is adapt, such as in the tech industry, where competition requires constant evolution. "And the network that most tech companies are looking to utilize for the future is the Metaverse," he writes.[3]

Fernandez cites Bill Gates's prediction for the network: that employees should expect their organizations to transition to Metaverse meetings in two to three years. He adds, "Hardware will continue to improve, and as it does, there will be large-scale adoption of the technology."[4]

Now is the time to consider the basis of our organizations through the lens of the next technological revolution. To become an early adopter of the Metaverse is to say, "We no longer allow panic to drive our business decisions; instead, we cling to principles that make us transcendent in our respective industries, and we move forward—intentionally."

IN BRIEF

Shedding the cost of physical real estate has an enormous impact on a company's bottom line. Not only that, but profitability is also enhanced by all the other benefits of a thoughtfully constructed Metaverse culture: collaboration, employee buy-in, and so on.

Image courtesy of Virbela

2

THE GREAT
EQUALIZER 2.0

Access to Do Good Work

"In this house, we work hard, Jason," my mother would say.

Growing up in a socioeconomically disadvantaged home, I learned the values of perseverance, work ethic, and discipline at a young age. Though we were lacking financially, we were abundant in identity, integrity, and self-respect. We learned what we could live without, even shared what we didn't need, and gave back to our community—which opened my eyes to the fact that there were people with different and more urgent needs than ours.

One of my earliest childhood memories is shoveling snow as a little boy, with raw hands and cheeks, in the icy streets of

Lawrence, Massachusetts, to make some extra money. I had never met my father, as he was not living with us. The public schools in Lawrence were under-resourced, overcrowded, and had started to develop a reputation for danger, drugs, and under-performance, so my mother worked hard to put me through private school. She wanted her son to have the opportunities she'd never experienced—opportunities that can emerge from attending great schools with small class sizes. Through a combination of her savings, my scholarships, and once I was old enough to work, a few of my summer checks, I was able to attend The Pike School in Andover, Massachusetts, and later a private secondary school.

My mother and I shared one common goal: to get me into college so I could make connections and get a better job than I could without an education. Even during my most unruly days as a kid, my mother's vision for my life remained in the forefront of my mind: access to college, access to resources, access to an abundant life.

I'll never forget when I almost sullied our plan. During my seventh-grade year, I was suspended from school for being untruthful to a teacher, ultimately threatening my scholarship and good standing. I've never seen such disappointment in my mother's eyes. That day made me realize that some have the privilege of having resources, while others have the privilege of being challenged, with the opportunity to build survival skills, get creative, and persevere through difficulties. The latter was the case for me. Such was the gift that life gave to my mother and me—*challenge* would shape my values and appreciation for work for the rest of my life.

The New Great Equalizer

Education has long been described as the great equalizer. However, in my experience, that has never been the case. If it was, every child would attend a safe school with sufficient funding and be offered equal opportunities to succeed. Throughout my childhood, I watched my mother experience the struggle many parents face: fight for educational access or fall behind.

My mother dreamed past societal barricades for me. She sacrificed her own desires so I could have more—not because she believed money is everything, but because she understood that money affords opportunity. Little did I know, adopting my mother's paradigm would eventually shape the way I do business.

While my mother could never give me a trust fund, she did teach me the value of educational resources and gave me the space to hone my strengths and improve my weaknesses. While some kids were lavished with material items—new school clothes every August, round-trip vacations to exciting locations for spring break, or cars for graduation—I was taught the value of hard work, and planted in an environment to cultivate that value. These values would shape my later business pursuits and make me a prime candidate to embrace the Metaverse.

Though I could never articulate this as a young person, *inclusive* access would be a key driver in my business decisions, making me more "meta-minded" than I would ever realize. I would come to embrace a business model that would make the future workforce more inclusive than ever before.

In answer to the question, "Can the Metaverse be more equitable than the physical world?" Jim Witte, professor of sociology and anthropology at George Mason University, agrees that it is a possibility, saying we can't expect inequities and exploitation to just disappear overnight, but the Metaverse's ability to bring educational opportunities to those who would otherwise not have such access is a tool for good.[1]

Replying to the same question, Nada Stirratt, vice president of Meta Platforms, Inc. (dba as Meta; it is famously known for Facebook), says that while the Metaverse does present a unique opportunity to overcome divisions in both physical and digital spaces, it will take intention and planning to achieve the equitable accessibility, safety, and opportunity it promises. Stirratt emphasizes, "It is critical that the Metaverse is designed inclusively from its very inception. This will require representation and leadership from experts across academia, policy, and other fields to develop technologies to inform future best practices and governance principles."[2]

The rise of Metaverse workplaces, where people can interact in a three-dimensional environment using virtual and augmented reality technologies, holds the potential to bring job opportunities to people in developing nations and enable broader economic access for more of us, no matter where we live.

By eliminating the need for physical offices and commutes, Metaverse workplaces allow individuals in remote or rural areas to access job opportunities that previously may not have been available to them. Not only that, greater flexibility and access to new and innovative industries could create new opportunities for people with diverse skill sets and backgrounds. Moreover, when work is no longer tied to or dependent upon physical location, employers in tight labor markets are able to fill important roles by accessing larger applicant and talent pools in diverse geographic (and oftentimes less costly) markets.

Challenges include access to technology, internet infrastructure, digital literacy, and privacy and security that must be addressed so we can ensure Metaverse workplaces are safe and accessible to all users. Despite these challenges, the potential benefits of Metaverse workplaces for job opportunities and economic access are significant. Meaning: as we move forward into the Metaverse, employees, contractors, and business owners will no longer be limited by the disqualifiers they've experienced in the traditional workplace. This will revolutionize hiring, in that candidates will no longer be disqualified by what they *lack*, because everyone now has equal access to jobs and training.

Furthermore, as the Metaverse becomes the new baseline, there will be less gatekeeping on potential employment opportunities. Contenders will have an equalized starting point, rendering traditional job qualifications, including college degrees, obsolete—placing growth potential back into the hands of eager workers who have only ever wanted a chance.

Perhaps the most triumphant feature of the Metaverse is that, as it surpasses education as "the great equalizer," it will provide a second chance for those whose school system failed them. **Those who were born into the privilege of challenge will finally get to experience the possibility of success.**

A Snapshot of Evolving Access

To those who have never experienced the Metaverse, its functions and equipment are hard to conceptualize. Those who have likened it to a video game are correct in their comparison, except that as a work environment, it's much more *real*.

Avatars can explore virtual sites and campuses, like the one at OMNUS or eXp, in real time. Users create simulations of themselves and use them to navigate the platform, most often using a computer or tablet. Once inside the network, users have access to infinite connections and destinations. During a break, after hours, or as part of a team-building exercise, they can meet with other avatars and explore virtual liaisons, attending simulated concerts, digital art exhibits, or avatar sporting events. One of my favorite community activities is hanging out on a speedboat, making waves in the pixelated lake. The design of this virtual sphere and its limitless functions are ingenious, comical, and creative—a combination that may delight employees yet inspire resistance, skepticism, and fear in the minds of conventional business owners.

If you are the type who prefers routine, finds comfort in a physical work environment, and resists introducing elements of fun into the workplace, I'd venture to guess I've already lost your attention. But I'm sorry to say—that traditional vision of the workplace is not sustainable. In the upcoming decades, any organization that does not plan to join the virtual workforce will fall behind. Industry leaders, academia, and the medical field are realizing this already—and leaning into the opportunities the Metaverse provides.

Take Fisk University in Nashville, Tennessee, for example. In 2021, Fisk invested in a virtual training cadaver lab as opposed to a multimillion-dollar physical facility that required costly real estate. Through this decision, the Metaverse made scientific learning more affordable and accessible to Fisk's premed and biology students.[3]

One of the professors' primary concerns regarding the Metaverse is the cost of virtual reality content licenses and equipment, not to mention the commitment to provide faculty with the training they require to deliver Metaverse courses. There is also still a gap in the creation of Metaverse learning materials—something that will evolve with time. Still, with the overwhelming popularity of digital and audio textbooks in the last decade and students' more recent gravitation to remote learning, there's little downside to learning about virtual teaching methods that will be the way of the future.

I would give parallel advice to business owners: all opportunities to expand reside in leadership's commitment to learning and investing in proper resources and technology. Some small- to medium-sized businesses are choosing to move forward in baby steps—they have downsized their physical footprint to smaller offices that host virtual experiences and headset labs. This option limits the risk of equipment loss that most employers take on when purchasing gear for their employees. All movement in this direction serves the interest of scaling.

Larger companies can expect that keeping brick-and-mortar offices open will exceed the combined cost of financed computers, Metaverse equipment, and licensure for the virtual space. Reallocation of these funds could go toward 24/7 access to advanced Metaverse-trained teams who can train and troubleshoot remote processes, or they could be poured back into the service professionals by increasing compensation in a manner that is disruptive to the rest of the industry.

Though this snapshot of evolving access may appear foreign or strange, never underestimate the power of gradual change. As schools and organizations provide Metaverse hubs, employees and students can explore the platform of the future. This invites them to dream of new ways of learning and operating in the workforce. The impact of integrating the Metaverse in the Western world parallels the introduction of high-speed Internet 2.0 in developing nations.

This experience was relevant to one gentleman to whom I was introduced by a fellow eXp World Holdings, Inc. board member. A native and resident of Ghana, where high-speed connection was unavailable in individual homes, Johnson was an avid technologist and was amazed by eXp's approach to business and office space and, more importantly, the connection that it enabled among people otherwise separated by great distance, culture, language, and more. Sensing his excitement, I invited him to join us for one of our weekly Friday morning company-wide meetings in our metaverse auditorium. At the time, eXp was operational in the US alone, so when Johnson took to the virtual stage to share a bit about his background, his country, and his passions, it represented in my mind our first step toward becoming a global company. There was one catch: in order for Johnson to attend and participate in the meeting, he needed to drive four hours to a Ghanaian internet café in order to establish an internet connection sufficient to power the platform. Johnson stayed beyond his own introduction and for the rest of the entire meeting, immersing himself in a collaborative workspace where people from global markets could come together to hear updates and share stories about their professional and personal lives. The relationships, skills, and opportunities made possible by such technology had the potential to change the trajectories of lives and careers forever.

Once the use of the Metaverse becomes more globally prevalent, we will begin to see users liberated in infinite ways—to explore the terrain of digital liaisons, to be considered for roles without the limitations of traditional biases, and to evolve into the students, professionals, and people they desire to be.

IN BRIEF

Education was once called the great equalizer; now the Metaverse can be that too. It offers a level playing field and access to employment that transcends geographic divides.

Image courtesy of Virbela

3

TRANSPARENCY AND LIFTING THE CURTAIN

More Human than Avatar

One of my family's more devastating realities was that my father abandoned our family both physically and financially before I was even born. This left my mother to persevere alone through cobbling together graveyard shifts at the hospital and working tenuous social work cases to keep food on our table.

I was reminded of those years of struggle when I transitioned from law, a profession with an excellent salary and benefits, to a start-up where I wasn't paying myself or being paid a salary. For the first two years with eXp, I had to make sacrifices that would benefit the company long-term. I focused on bringing the skills I could lend to the table and watching the vision transform. The costs of entrepreneurship were paid out of my pocket, in my case.

That's the truth of business ownership—investing time, mental energy, and resources into something you care about that could fail. In the beginning, the bottom fell out more often than it didn't, but I was challenged to grow and learn from those experiences—luckily, with the help of my mentors and colleagues.

I don't hesitate to share these experiences, because I know that the lessons I gained from those times of struggle are the ones staff and colleagues find the most affirming. When we relay these stories, we are more than avatars behind a screen— we are *real*.

I emphasize what I've learned as much as I can because being a transparent leader requires honesty about times when we were *human*—times when we couldn't make ends meet, succumbed to poor judgment, made uneducated decisions, worked against our values, or tragically lost everything—for no sensible reason at all.

Human stories weave trust and culture into the fabric of a work environment. They are even more crucial to a digital work-force. Luckily, the Metaverse model offers versatile connection where we can see each other's faces, hear each other's voices, and shoulder each other's burdens from across the globe.

Beyond "Top-down" Leadership

Mike Kappel, founder of Patriot Software and a *Forbes* maga-zine contributor, defines transparency in business as "the process of being open, honest, and straightforward about various company operations." Kappel goes on to say, "Transparent companies share information relating to performance, small business revenue, internal processes, sourcing, pricing, and business values."[1]

Kappel's definition rings true for me because it challenges the idea of "top-down" leadership—a management style defined by unhealthy power dynamics, gatekeeping information, and limited access to corporate executives. Over the past few decades, there has been a seismic shift in leadership styles that has taken us away from the traditional, hierarchical model and toward something more collaborative.

At the heart of this shift lies a recognition of the importance of teamwork. In today's fast-paced and complex business environment, no one person can be expected to have all the answers or make all the decisions. Instead, organizations are turning to more inclusive and participatory models, where employees are encouraged to work together to find solutions and drive innovation.

Changing demographics have also contributed to the shift toward a more collaborative leadership style. Younger generations entering the workforce bring with them different values and expectations—including a desire for greater autonomy and flexibility. Leaders who can adapt to these changing expectations are more likely to succeed in attracting and retaining top talent.

Technology has played a key role in this evolution, too. With the rise of social media and other digital platforms, leaders have new tools at their disposal for communicating with their followers and building more direct, two-way relationships. By leveraging these channels, they can create a more engaged and connected workforce that is better equipped to handle the demands of the modern world. The Metaverse expands upon that new dynamic and takes it further than ever before.

Decades in the traditional workforce taught me the detriments of command-and-control hierarchies, where supervisors keep a tight rein on information and the messages that filter down through middle management. Because of communication gaps in these workspaces, employees often experience training setbacks, insufficient work resources (or information), inadequate feedback or quarterly reviews, restricted growth opportunities, and a lack of job security. As a result, employee satisfaction and retention rates drop due to feelings of powerlessness, frustration, and distrust.

This is why I firmly believe in a "bottom-up" management style, where employees hold power through stock ownership. Employees with a stake in their company inevitably possess a distinct mindset that fosters a culture of responsibility and shared purpose that can yield positive outcomes for both the workers and the company they collectively own. They have a heightened sense of accountability for their job performance, as well as that of their colleagues, which drives them to work more efficiently. This culture is exemplified in companies like Publix, the grocery store chain that is also the largest employee-owned company operating in the US. After being with Publix for twelve months, all employees are eligible to join the company's employee stock ownership plan (ESOP). The company has been ranked as one of the best companies to work for in America, thanks in part to its employee ownership model. San Francisco–based waste management company Recology is another successful company that is entirely owned by its 3,600-plus employees, having started its ESOP program back in 1986.

The notion of employee ownership is relevant to a wide swath of service industries, and one of my current pursuits is finding innovative ways to apply this principle to other service professions, such as law firms, to the benefit of both the service professionals and their clients.

Photo courtesy of Virbela

I believe extending ownership opportunities through a Metaverse model (or even in a traditional setting) is one of the most generative and effective benefits a company can offer its employees. I enjoy thinking about or discussing the advantages of scaling on a remote platform; digitally spanning geographic regions; leaving labor shortages in the dust; and paying employees more because a remote workspace enables companies to "cut the fat." I also enjoy talking about how to position a company to become the primary competitor in its respective industry and dominate in the digital space.

However, what excites me most is talking about how individuals can foster company growth while at the same time creating a "dividend culture" where people *want* to continue to be shareholders. In companies with a dividend culture, every single employee or stakeholder wants to be a leader; they value troubleshooting problems instead of running from them; they are personally invested in the company because *it is theirs.*

"What's mine is ours," eXp agents say, whether they've been with the company for five months or five years. Naturally, they view their investments a little differently than if they were just on-the-clock employees—they incorporate a healthy perfectionism and a sense of deliberate contribution, essentially the guardians at the gate.

The benefit of ownership in a Metaverse model is being able to process the ups and downs as a unified front. When our organization misses the mark, we face disappointment together and get right back up again. When we succeed, the slice of the proverbial pie is all the sweeter because—beyond profit—we generously celebrate that we have each other to share it with.

When business owners with shared values recognize how effectively the Metaverse can drive connection within an organization, they too can get creative about facilitating professional development, mentorship, and transparency across the globe.

I anticipate the Metaverse will render "top-down" leadership models extinct. Traditionally inclined leaders won't fully benefit from the platform's functionality without a shift in perspective about its most flexible and engaging features.

On Metaverse campuses, the work experience is immersive—it requires deliberation, presence, and attentiveness. Meetings invite transparency and communication from employees, and even off the clock, they remain on-site to play games, attend virtual parades, or meet with social interest groups. Remaining detached or disengaged would be an intentional decision—a choice that would deprive both the leader and the community of an excellent development experience.

Numbered are the days that workers will be governed by hierarchal assemblies, exclusive management teams, and company politics. In the Metaverse, professionals will prioritize working for executives who lead with integrity, listen attentively, are willing to take public accountability for their shortcomings, and who attribute credit to others for collective achievements and success.

Just like a brick-and-mortar building cannot compensate for lack of security or stable company culture—*nothing* compensates for lack of quality leadership. It doesn't matter if salaries are high, PTO is generous, and benefits packages are promising. If those advantages come at the cost of an employee being able to develop—or if they are thrust into a high-pressure, imbalanced environment—they will not stay. They will go where their time, efforts, and energy are appreciated.

Workers may well find their needs met most abundantly in Metaverse workspaces—defined by collaborative leadership, vibrant digital communities, and boundless possibilities for growth.

Trust Is a Two-Way Street

The Metaverse excels as a vehicle for values. At eXp, for example, maintaining the strong interpersonal fibers was a high priority from the start, and versatile meeting spaces gave the platform a chance to prove its worth. As teams assembled in virtual boardrooms, chatted on the roofs of skyscrapers, climbed aboard digital speedboats, and joined in other surreal experiences and environments, executives created an authentic bond with their teams. They learned that a digital space could foster qualities like clarity, honesty, authenticity, transparency, creativity—and fun. And I speculated that what was true for eXp's campus could be true for every virtual company.

Depending on an organization's interpretation of "transparency," the unique functions of the platform can serve in dynamic ways. I have seen that the adaptability of the Metaverse can bolster evolving work processes—and communicating about those processes. Innovative functions help refine best practices, train employees effectively, and deliver information and resources to teams. The digitization of these functions can help you to exceed your goals as an organization—positioning you to grow past what you may have believed was possible.

The Metaverse can also help establish trust.

In a virtual workspace, it's possible to cultivate an environment where participants across countries and continents feel recognized, safe, and confident enough in the leadership that factors like location, language differences, and work history are no barrier to performance and worker satisfaction. This notion is bolstered by the work of Jason Kujanen, human principal capitalist at TriNet. As part of his graduate thesis, he made the case for transparency being the most important cultural attribute for an effective remote work environment. He explains, "This is because transparency is paramount to employee engagement. And, as we know, employee engagement is paramount to a business's productivity. A majority of the remote employees I interviewed for my thesis stated that they appreciated knowing their managers were easily accessible for questions or urgent matters."[2]

Kujanen's findings are consistent with my experience in the Metaverse: businesses grow in satisfaction, retention, and revenue when they work hand in hand with every employee, no matter their position in the industry, company, or team. The fact that organizations now have access to a digital network supporting these connections is revolutionary.

As organizations shuttle into the future of the Metaverse and explore what it means across industries, we can confidently do so, knowing that transparency will foster the evolution of companies and propagate the trust that fuels a positive company culture.

Lifting the Curtain

One tenet for a productive work culture is summed up in the maxim: "Get things out from behind the curtain." What comes to mind when I hear this phrase is the "Great and Powerful Oz," who, from beneath the concealment of a velvet curtain, was deceptive about his identity and intentions for the people of The Emerald City. Like any influential leader, Oz was a charismatic visionary with exceptional power and the weighty choice of how he would use it. As many do, Oz stumbled into abuse of authority when presented with the option to prioritize his position over honest relationships with the people.

There's always a tinge of fear in top-down management structures when the "great and powerful boss" has something to say. Employees gather in the boardroom, nervous that such meetings indicate some kind of sinister writing on the wall. In the Metaverse, I have wanted to eliminate this response by any means possible—an effort that has largely influenced us to conduct meetings in the most unusual places: virtual pirate ships, digital islands, performance lounges, or soccer fields. Changing the setting to a fun place seems to automatically alleviate much of the fear.

The reality is—meetings don't have to be formal to be effective. Our ability to customize a Metaverse campus to support these interactions has positively influenced the health of our culture and the overall satisfaction of our employees. And because our executives don't believe in gatekeeping information, our employees don't come into company gatherings on high alert.

The benefit of avatar and video meetings is that everyone involved can engage in real time. When a leader hops on a live broadcast to communicate a message to the global community, both local and international teams can respond by liking, commenting, and sharing the update. They can also engage in private chat conversations to process what they are hearing. This is an excellent tool for one-on-ones between seasoned team members and newer employees, who might have questions. The Metaverse makes these meetings user-friendly so those who are less technologically savvy don't feel the exhaustion that is typical in virtual meetings.

Kevin Eikenberry and Wayne Turmel examine this type of engagement in their book, *The Long-Distance Leader*. The authors write, "The richer the communication you have, the easier it is to build trust with others. Conversely, in the absence of the visual clues, the development of trust can be slowed or more easily broken."[3] I recognized their statement to be true in a physically distanced workplace, which is why I appreciate the capability of the Metaverse to support transparent communication, both one-on-one and global. In the Metaverse, visual cues are possible if you are also using your video camera (usually not the case) but most often replaced with other forms of feedback—tone of voice when someone turns on their microphone or use of emojis to express emotions.

In the Metaverse, "Step into my office . . ." need not be a thing. One, because you don't have brick-and-mortar offices; and two, because your global team members will have seen your face (and your avatar) enough to unanimously trust you (and approach you confidently in person). They will know that as a leader, you want your community to thrive. And you can thank the Metaverse for providing a virtual space with limitless options to do so—as you cultivate an environment of safety, connection, and transparency.

Leadership Cultivates Trust

One man's ego can bring down a kingdom. We see this all the time in business.

While the "you eat what you kill" mentality has been successful for many organizations, and real estate can be as brutal as any other industry, I decided early on that it was valuable and important to me to work with people who possessed humility—and to then develop them to operate with integrity and transparency.

One of the most defining challenges of my career has been learning to identify (and own) when we've mistakenly placed people in positions of leadership who are "company killers." We know leaders are made and not born—that even those with the best intentions don't always deliver with great execution, that there's always room for improvement, and that we need to be transparent about our blind spots. This type of leadership requires honesty and consistency, which will, in turn, cultivate trust.

Countless opportunities exist to hide behind power in business: to withhold information, skirt the truth, not own mistakes, and not operate from a place of authenticity. But at what cost do we give in to this temptation?

When trust between leadership and employees is eroded, the company is at a disadvantage. No one operates well out of fear. When power dynamics incite tension, awkwardness, or anxiety among workers, rumors and division abound. Employees with honest, professional values find themselves living in a difficult tension: be transparent about their misgivings with leadership or forfeit the career that feeds their family because of personal standards. A decent person can only stay in this impossible position for so long before they quit—ultimately costing the organization upstanding employees.

Alternatively, when these professionals are included in

impactful decisions and significant changes, their morale remains positive regardless of whether they agree. And if they are dissatisfied, they will be more willing to trust leadership in times of uncertainty if they are confident that they are being given adequate information.

But what about matters that arguably need to be confidential? Obviously, not all industries are the same. What applies to real estate may not apply to software development, healthcare, or law firms. In certain work cultures, employees might be more ambivalent or confused by an onslaught of information if it doesn't directly pertain to them, their role, or a tangible vision of the organization's future. Identical values can present differently across industries, organizations, and teams. Trust-building might look different between a supervisor and a new employee versus between a salesperson and a client. Still, a commitment to honesty and clarity drives these interactions. Both speak to the integrity of an organization and the transparency of its culture.

Universally, companies are set up for success when employees can see and engage with their leaders regularly. Because remote environments can feel vast, leaders must choose and implement methods of communication that bolster the values of their organization. The efforts that turn the dial can be as small as sending monthly updates, hosting virtual quarterly Q&As, or encouraging engagement through polling and global discourse.

When employees feel included in significant decisions and large-scale changes, they demonstrate more confidence in leadership. As a result, executives can interpret what incentivizes their workforce—enabling them to facilitate a transcendent culture among industry competitors.

Three Fundamentals of Virtual Transparency
1. CONNECTION EQUALS CONFIDENCE

Since the 2020 global pandemic, the landscape of our society has been marked by disconnection. Internationally, we have faced political upheaval, economic strife, war, and shifting work modalities. A company's ability to thrive has depended upon their ability to maintain their social structure after transitioning to a remote model.

Successful virtual companies understand that connection equals confidence. They offer meaningful ways for employees to interact with their colleagues and leaders at a distance.

While connection can somewhat be achieved through Internet 2.0, the potential connectivity of a Metaverse model far surpasses that of the brick-and-mortar workplace.

Operating as an avatar in a digital environment requires a level of presence that *feels* physical. Unlike the video interface of Zoom, controlling the motions of a simulation and responding in real time is as interactive as an on-site experience. Avatars meet, shake hands, fist bump, stroll, sail, and fly together.

This not only makes distanced professional environments more engaging, but it also establishes a (paradoxically) high level of humanity between colleagues. It might come as a surprise that meetings hosted on virtual tropical islands build trust—but the notion that work and play can coexist is essential when cultivating trust in professional settings.

When employees feel connected to their leaders and teammates in small ways, they will be more likely to be transparent with significant matters—presenting opportunities for more durable relationships in the workplace that foster a sense of safety.

2. SMALL TALK MAKES A BIG IMPACT

Break room conversations can be immediate morale boosters: catching coworkers up on the family, contesting over fantasy football leagues, celebrating birthdays, and commemorating milestones are invaluable to company culture. Because watercooler gatherings have been a workplace staple for generations, businesses are reluctant to give up their physical offices—not understanding that the Metaverse makes for an even more dynamic break room experience.

Whether in the virtual mountains or in bustling digital cities, the Metaverse gives users the opportunity to connect anywhere imaginable. Companies that prioritize connection will find limitless ways to create their conversations virtually. These simulated get-togethers help employees feel like they are not isolated from the community.

The opportunities for small talk are endless in the Metaverse and can help build authentic connections among employees who would otherwise remain disengaged. Trust and transparency are built in environments where colleagues can relax and interact informally, and the Metaverse excels at creating those moments.

3. OPENNESS IS NOT WITHOUT GOVERNANCE

Within every virtual organization, two things need to exist to foster a safe work environment: freedom and order.

Though these two sound like opposites, in reality they work in tandem to keep employees safe. HR departments are better positioned than ever to track productivity, document time clock disparities, and monitor inappropriate work conversations.

That said, micromanaging and invading employee chats without reason doesn't yield a culture of trust and transparency. If anything, it breeds anxiety, contempt, and disdain for the work at hand—and for the leadership that enforces such measures.

I like to trust people to make their own judgment calls. I want to encourage transparency, not expose people just because we can. When stripped of their dignity, no person stays at a workplace for long. That level of trust depends on establishing transparent relationships with new hires from the start. After they've made it through a thorough vetting process that confirms their values align with those of the organization, there is good reason to expect they will not break your trust.

That said, the virtual frontier needs parameters for a healthy, stable environment. Every remote workspace should be intentional about creating a Code of Conduct and reviewing it regularly as it relates to employee relations and security. In chapter 4, we will go into the risks of working and sharing our social lives in the digital space.

○ ○ ○ ○ ○

The Metaverse provides a space that makes *realness* possible. The environment amply supports digital connections—even when teams are countries apart. Through virtual business meetings, boat rides, pirate ship explorations, and conferences, we experience limitless ways to bond with teammates, collaborate on projects, evaluate best practices, and learn from industry leaders.

Through these interactions, we get to see the values of an organization lived out: integrity, community, collaboration, and transparency.

IN BRIEF

The Metaverse enables a greater flow of information within a company and access to leadership—*if* that is part of the company's values.

Image courtesy of Virbela

4

BUILDING A SECURE WORKPLACE

First, Do No Harm

Had my employers placed a biometric wristband on me during my early years working in law, they would have learned pretty quickly that I was miserable. These devices can detect subtle "tells" of employee engagement, such as eye movements, body shifts, and facial expressions. When we get excited, for example, our pupils dilate and the corners of our mouth pull back; when we are in a deep state of "flow," our breathing rate changes and our brow furrows into an expression of focus. For a number of years, I suspect I displayed no such signs of excitement or flow while I sat at my desk.

As technology propels humanity into a limitless future, wearable devices can detect subtle cues in a person's tone of voice, body language, and social interactions. With this innovation, we can now monitor not only our own movements and habits, but also begin to infer the thoughts and motivations of those around us.

Biometric wearables have the potential to revolutionize the way we understand human behavior and communication, providing exceptional insights into the details of social interaction. By tracing subliminal signals, these devices allow for a level of analysis that was previously impossible, granting us a window into the deeper layers of human behavior.

From the boardroom to the classroom, the implications of this technology are vast and far-reaching. With the ability to monitor subtle cues in real time, organizations can now gain a deeper understanding of the intentions and motivations of their employees. If applied with inclusivity in mind, biometric data could help employers better accommodate those who struggle with learning disorders, mental health difficulties, or physical disabilities by giving them unique support that sets them up for success.

As with any technology, both potential benefits and concerns arise with the use of biometrics in the workplace. While some view it as a powerful tool for unlocking the mysteries of human behavior, others worry about the implications of such invasive monitoring.

The distinguishing feature between intrusion and safety is, I believe, a deep, clearly articulated, and determined commitment to trust in an organization. This is not a matter of sentiment, but commercial reality: it is what our employees, clients, business partners, and the wider public expect from us. As digital safety and sustainability expert Tiffany Xingyu Wang puts it, "Trust is a strategic growth driver and brand differentiator." She goes on to say, "In other words, safety, privacy, and inclusion, the three pillars of digital trust, are not only for good but also for growth."[1]

The Fear of Big Brother

Regardless of the liberating opportunities of the Metaverse, a 2022 study by ExpressVPN (makers of privacy and security software) demonstrated that out of 1,500 employees surveyed, 57 percent are apprehensive about transitioning to a Metaverse environment—primarily due to the potential trackability of their biometric data.[2] Though these workers are incentivized by the chance to design personalized workspaces, ditch their morning commute, save money on fuel, establish work-life balance, expand their network on a global scale, learn innovative ways of doing business, and have access to more and better professional opportunities—they fear for their personal privacy.

Data collected in the same study details that employers would indeed use the Metaverse to monitor their personnel more closely—especially those employers aiming toward global expansion. At least 40 percent of 1,500 employers surveyed confirmed they would record all meetings; upward of 35 percent revealed their plans for tracking real-time location, screen movements, and browser history; roughly 30 percent intend to observe engagement with applications and personal downloads, biometrics, and eye movement; just above 20 percent plan to take this surveillance one step further by tracking body metrics (blinking, breathing, pupil dilations, facial expressions, and physical motions).[3]

While the revelations in this study might give skeptical employees pause about the intentions of Metaverse employers, the most intriguing part of this research was that it proved the apprehensions of these employees to be exaggerated. For example, 51 percent of employees feared real-time location tracking—yet only 39 percent of employers would utilize that function. Fifty percent of employees worried about real-time screen monitoring—yet only 39 percent of employers plan to track screen activity. Up to 40 percent of employees worried about biometric data tracking—yet only 31 percent of employers plan to implement the tracking of this information. In fact, the only metric where employees *underestimated* trackability in the workplace was in regard to recorded meetings (ironically a Metaverse function that has more universal pros than cons).[4]

Notably, less than 2 percent of participants in the ExpressVPN survey already work in a Metaverse environment. For that reason, this study alone is not an accurate representation of the reality of Metaverse work models. It is, however, a good depiction of expectations, concerns, and intentions on the part of individuals and organizations alike.

Having acquainted myself with the functions and the trajectory of the Metaverse for over a decade, I can see that we have good reason to be wary. The era of Internet 2.0 taught us a valuable lesson that prioritizing growth over safety in platform development can have dire consequences for individuals. As we reflect on the recent past, it becomes clear that the emphasis on rapid growth and user acquisition led to a disregard for potential dangers and vulnerabilities within these platforms. For evidence of the impact of social media on society when left unchecked, we need look no further than the January 6, 2021, attack on the United States Capitol Building. In the years leading up to this event, online communities had become increasingly polarized and radicalized, with extremist groups using social media platforms to organize and spread propaganda. Many critics argue that this problem could have been mitigated if tech companies had implemented stronger safety and privacy protocols in the early days of social media. By failing to do so, they allowed the uncontrolled spread of dangerous ideologies and misinformation to fester and grow, ultimately culminating in events like those of the 2021 insurrection, triggering national upheaval and political division. This toxic environment was allowed to thrive due to a lack of meaningful regulation and safeguards, as well as a failure to acknowledge the potential dangers of rampant social media use.

In the words of Tiffany Xingyu Wang, "Technology brings us this fascinating world we live in today, but because safety was an afterthought in Web 2.0, we ended up where we are today."[5] I would argue that the events of January 6 were not an isolated incident, but rather a symptom of a larger problem: the failure of tech companies to prioritize user safety and privacy over profits and engagement. Every service sector organization that considers adopting a Metaverse work environment faces the same ethical imperative now of taking responsibility for its role in creating these environments and taking meaningful steps toward implementing robust safety and privacy protocols.

I anticipate that in the near future we will have an international body with the remit to ensure privacy and safety policies in every Metaverse environment. In the meantime, I recommend that every corporation takes the initiative to implement safeguards to ensure a secure workplace.

The Seven Safeguards of a Secure Workspace
1. SAFEGUARDING THE INDIVIDUAL

In the Metaverse, there will be one unified bank of data across platforms—personified by one's avatar. The pixelated "blockhead" that has represented me throughout the years is an embodiment of millions of data points. My history, clicks, chats, and digital activity are centralized in one place.

The concept is similar to the current digital profile. Consider the idea of private accounts across platforms: computer, application, email, social media, financial, healthcare—the list goes on. These siloed "data banks" have disconnected interfaces, but on the back end they are inextricably linked. If law enforcement were to intervene at any point, or if bad actors were to operate a phishing scheme, they would look to the connection points of these profiles.

From a tech perspective, the increase of interconnectedness across platforms means an increase of usability, traceability, and more strongly defined digital footprints. Even in the spaces where these profiles do not touch, they still chronologize and archive user activity, making every digital move we've ever made online recoverable and banked confidential information even more available than is immediately obvious.

These advances are as revolutionary as they are precarious—and will remain so across industries where confidentiality breaches pose more of a threat. For example, Metaverse tracking in medical workspaces will modernize the industry by creating more accurate vital signs tracking and data collection, as well as thorough documentation for medical records. At the same time, this model puts the patient and the provider more at risk if a breach were to take place and a patient's data was to become compromised. There will be different levels of security required in different industries. The ramifications of leaked data in areas such as banking, law enforcement, legal consultation, or behavioral health could be catastrophic. As business owners transition into a Metaverse workspace, they will need to consider the costs of adequate security measures for their unique environment. Some of these measures include the implementation of blockchain-based authentication, multifactor and multisignature login requirements, and defense against malware, ransomware, bad actors, hackers, and identity thieves.

2. SAFEGUARDING INFORMATION

With evolving data collection comes an increased need for security. Beyond protecting employee and client information through security programs, business owners need to have strategic processes for the exchange and protection of digital information.

According to professional services powerhouse PwC, "The Metaverse will need rules to govern security, interactions among users, tax collection, data governance, regulatory compliance and more. These rules are not yet settled, but already, Metaverse platforms can pose new governance and security challenges."[6] Employers need to plan around the possibilities of cyberattacks and vet their own security playbooks and those of their vendors and partners accordingly for the protection of employees and clients.

Beyond the safeguarding of information in a secure digital work environment is the protection *against* misinformation. Despite the profound benefits of trackability in the Metaverse, data in the wrong hands creates room for distortion and extortion. Implementation of identity-confirming technology, multifactor authentication, encryption-based data storage, or safe protection services offered through trusted vendors will assuage fears of data mining and protect personnel from an array of cyber injuries.

3. SAFEGUARDING SOFTWARE

The Metaverse as a space of navigation, exploration, and commerce is not indestructible. Like any major global resource, it will need to be protected against design malfunctions and weak entry points for bad actors. Cyberbullying is the devil we know, but in a new digital sphere, those who experience software breaches via exposure to lewd, violent, or offensive images could be severely traumatized. This is where calling upon trained technological guardians will be paramount.

Ideally, every organization will have a team of Metaverse-savvy software experts who test and procure network safety. Additionally, companies should partner with mental health and medical support teams that specialize in digital traumatization. Not all of these teams have to be human; AI will especially come in handy by managing processes that protect digital programs. Where humans fail, these bots will be encoded to identify, troubleshoot, and resolve software issues *before* they lead to security breaches. Alongside AI will be third-party vendors bringing a human touch to software management and privacy protocols.

While securing the Metaverse at large will depend upon legislation to keep users safe, corporate leaders can assist in this common goal by maintaining a platform of functionality and top-notch program protection.

4. SAFEGUARDING HARDWARE

Eye, facial, breath, and motion recognition are not without their purposes; however, a higher influx of identifying data means a higher risk of impersonators. Similar to the hacking of computers, virtual reality (VR) headsets and other Metaverse-related gear are also vulnerable to hacking. As PwC points out, "[the Metaverse] will likely offer new attack surfaces for malicious actors . . . three-dimensional experiences could make some cyberattacks deeply traumatic."[7]

These attacks can become especially harmful for those with mental or physical disabilities—especially if they experience symptoms triggered by certain lighting, sounds, colors, or concepts. Additional injuries due to hacked gear include identity theft and fraudulent financial activity, putting people at risk of emotional damages, or worse, putting people in physical danger *outside* of the Metaverse.

According to Eric Wang from Harvard's Labor and Employment Lab, "Current VR functionalities that track a person's head and hand movements can be used to identify the user with up to 95 percent accuracy. As a result, VR tracking data can serve as a digital fingerprint that makes it impossible to maintain your anonymity."[8] Thus, hardware will be safeguarded from impersonators, and profiles/avatars will be at little risk of responding to hackers or general users. Our headsets and other gear will intimately know us through biometric tracking.

Safeguarding these functions will rely largely upon preventive measures: the thorough and accurate programming of gear; utilization of AI and third-party vendors for additional layers of protection; and most importantly, a trusted team of technological guardians that will support the organization if the technology itself should fail.

5. SAFEGUARDING "THE HEDGE"

One of the primary appeals of the Metaverse as a workspace is interoperability: the capability of *any* avatar to access *any* digital site on the map of the Metaverse. As in the physical world, individuals can find, travel to, and roam the cyber headquarters and meeting rooms of an organization freely (unless otherwise prohibited). Without a programmed "hedge of protection" surrounding the borders of a digital space, all companies are at risk for impostors, miscreants, or hackers to breach security systems and leak confidential data.

This is where the concept of a "virtual hedge" comes into play. These invisible workspace boundaries can be created through specific encoded rules around digital campuses, or the parameters within each site that are off-limits to certain personnel. The hedge keeps unwanted visitors *out* and secured data *in*—making your business a safe camp for employees and leadership to conduct their work without threat or interruption.

One of the largest providers of Metaverse work environments is Virbela. (Full disclosure: Virbela is one of the businesses under the eXp World Holdings umbrella.)[9] Its founder, Alex Howland, deals with questions of privacy and security with his corporate clients on a daily basis. "The challenge of the path forward is how do we provide those high-walled gardens for organizations who want it, but still find ways to easily jump between different parts of the global ecosystem of Virbela campuses?" he says. Using eXp as an example, "They have a campus that they use just for investor meetings, shareholder meetings. . . . Think about being able to jump between worlds—[they might] require SSO [single sign-in authentication] to get into, say, the realty part of the ecosystem, but they might want open access to the investor relations group," he adds.[10]

6. SAFEGUARDING THE GUARDIANS

One of the most critical steps we can take in preparation for the rollout of the Metaverse is adequately training and equipping technological teams to support scaling organizations. As it stands, leading technology experts have only dipped their toes into the potential of the Metaverse; the majority have not learned much beyond the complexities of the Internet 2.0.

Without forerunners in this field who are equipped with ample budgets, adequate gear, access to upgrades, and thorough training, Metaverse corporations will not be supported. If there was *one* place for an organization to budget outside of technological apparatus, it would be securing a knowledgeable tech team that can move an organization forward with its understanding of the new digital space, software, and evolving technological trends.

7. SAFEGUARDING SELF-GOVERNANCE

With the advantage of trackability, employers can know more about their workers than ever. As demonstrated throughout this chapter, *both* the employer and the employees of an organization can benefit from this transparency. That said, this last safeguard speaks more to leadership establishing a sense of trust in their organization as opposed to providing a technological solution.

Equipped with revolutionized tracking ability and data transparency, employers have even *more* reason to trust well-vetted employees. As we enter a platform that is more surveilled than ever before, business leaders are presented with the unique opportunity to create a sense of liberation, autonomy, and self-governance within the parameters of a "watched workspace."

When performance data is collected by leadership, they have

the opportunity to use that knowledge to develop their teams (as opposed to using it for leverage or disciplinary measures). It's less about the tracking of the data and more about what employers *do* with the information. An invasion of privacy is not an "invasion" if it is welcomed—in the sense that employees are receptive to feedback on their performance based on actual data, and have provided confirmation that they agree to their data being tracked. This dismantles the notion that any Metaverse employee is being "held captive" or under watch by the "eyes" of their organization.

Instead, performance numbers can be evaluated and used to position employees for more fulfilling work, higher earning potential, and longevity with an organization. This safeguarding of autonomy will facilitate trust between leadership and personnel—bolstered by evolving legislation regarding the Metaverse as it pertains to privacy and security.

Although currently much is to be determined in regard to the laws on digital privacy, healthy organizations stand as Metaverse forerunners and advocates for protected digital workspaces. We want our work to serve as an example for how to create a healthy professional environment while petitioning for revisions of existing laws.

The current regulations leave a great deal of interpretation up to legal officials, employers, and third-party data collectors. While this creates mixed feelings among Metaverse skeptics, some of the adaptable language in these laws is because, in part, the Metaverse is evolving faster than we can determine statutes around it. As biometric data collection becomes more of the norm in remote workspaces, public opinion will shift from reflecting what employees *fear* to be true about working in the Metaverse to what is *actually* true about utilizing trackability to facilitate a secure work environment.

Looking to Digital Pioneers

In the midst of the great digital transition from the Internet 2.0 to the Metaverse, employers will have digital pioneers to look up to—some that have thrived for more than a decade—in a "lawless land," simply because of strong company ethics. Leading businesses and their satisfied employees that have healthfully expanded their international Metaverse workforces can serve as a testament that the provision of certain personal information can be (paradoxically) liberating—and an entirely reasonable trade-off for the security, professional development, and career growth workers receive in return.

Privacy and safety are, when all is said and done, vital for profitability. Without sturdy protections and strong ethical guardrails, employees cannot feel safe. And if they don't feel safe, they cannot create the community in the Metaverse that is necessary to achieve success.

IN BRIEF

People fear that their privacy and safety will be threatened in the Metaverse (personal data mining and hacking, cyberbullying, etc.). These fears are well-grounded, so organizations must put safeguards in place to protect the individual, information, software, hardware, boundaries, and culture.

5

TOP-DOWN ACCOUNTABILITY

Bad Behavior in Cyberspace

The Metaverse is emerging in the midst of a most turbulent era. Arguably, the Western world has never been more divided or inflamed—and many of the flame points are intricately tangled with Big Tech. We are in the wake of Elon Musk's acquisition of Twitter (rebranded in 2023 as X), which sparked rampant speculation about the impact on the 2024 United States presidential elections, and even comparisons to the last days of Weimar Germany. Twitter has developed an outsized impact on public opinion and behavior, so it's little wonder that people are on the defensive.

The current environment does not help when it comes to relaying information about the Metaverse and what it will mean to exist and do business there. The general public fears the unknown, and a climate of many who do not yet understand what the Metaverse as a workplace will be like leaves ample room for fearmongering and uneducated criticism. Your organization and you must get ahead of misinformation and unfounded sentiment before investing your time, money, and resources in the digital space.

Right now, commentating on these matters is difficult; creating an accurate depiction of something potential users of the Metaverse have not yet experienced is challenging—a bit like building the plane while you are flying it. Fourteen years ago, when I described working in the Metaverse, people looked at me like I was crazy. Now, the expression has changed and includes a bit of fear driven by mistrust of this new virtual world and the kinds of behavior that may proliferate there, but also a recognition of its utility and its effectiveness at transforming enterprises in a manner that can catapult them over their competition.

We must put these hesitations in context by acknowledging the limitations of a conventional work model, founded on the notion that physical oversight ensures solid managerial practices and compliance training, as well as stellar behavior by all parties. However, the "tensions" regarding accountability in the Metaverse far more likely have more to do with a general fear of foundational changes as well as a lack of awareness of its versatile functions and applications.

At the most elementary level, many business owners and managers believe one needs eyes on employees to prevent bad behaviors such as bullying, sexual harassment, and simple work avoidance. And yet the notion that you need to be in physical proximity to someone in order to hold them accountable has been proven not to be the case.

Based on my own experience working in the legal profession and other traditional environments, being physically present inside a brick-and-mortar office building is no guarantee of accountability. Each working day, I would drink seven Diet Cokes—just so I could leave my desk, walk to the kitchen, go back to my desk, drink my soda, then get up again and go to the bathroom . . . seven times a day. I find it hard to believe that I'm the only one who has found ways to occupy themselves other than by tackling the tasks that await them at their desk.

Cyberloafing is defined in the Macmillan Dictionary as "using the internet where you work, during working hours, for activities that are not related to work." When employees are cyberloafing, they are noodling on social media accounts, checking personal emails, browsing through YouTube videos, and conducting other unproductive activities. This can happen in any workplace. A study from the Wisconsin School of Business at the University of Wisconsin-Madison estimates that, depending on the employee, the time spent cyberloafing can range from "3 hours a week to as much as 2.5 hours per day." Though employees with more conscientiousness and emotional stability are less likely to engage in cyberloafing, according to Professor Maria Triana, even a strong work ethic will not overcome cyberloafing "if they feel there is a lack of justice or fair treatment in the workplace." Therefore, she suggests that organizations not only focus "on those personal traits, but [create] a work environment where employees believe they are treated fairly and equitably."[1]

Nobody likes a micromanager—in-person or in-avatar.

We all know that energized supervisor who, in an on-site establishment, pops their head over the cubicle wall a little too often. They bring an unnecessary tension to meetings, leave no room for error when communicating expectations, address "pain points" through criticism only, and are impossible to approach about growth opportunities. While their militant methods may be effective at catching slackers (or forcing them to be ever more inventive in their slacking), they keep great employees on edge about everything from asking for time off, requesting guidance on team projects, or even taking bathroom breaks. Inevitably, they negatively impact company retention—because nobody wants to work around them!

"People have an amazing ability to live down to low expectations," say authors and entrepreneurs Jason Fried and David Heinemeier Hansson. "If you run your ship with the conviction that everyone's a slacker, your employees will put all their ingenuity into proving you right."[2]

If the accountability of your employees is truly dependent upon virtual or in-person babysitting, remote work is probably the least of your problems. And frankly, the larger danger in a Metaverse work environment is overperforming rather than underperforming. If you have populated your team with driven, passionate people and crafted an environment that cultivates their creativity and innovation, you are more likely to have to manage people out of excess than to spur them into activity. This is even more true when you have a global team, people working in multiple time zones and with different cultural norms around start and end times. In the Metaverse, someone is nearly always around to collaborate with. "How wonderful," you may be thinking. "Our employees will be so productive!" In fact, the "always-on" culture is a recipe for burnout. In this respect, leaders must set the tone and be accountable themselves. Be a role model, working sustainable hours. Use the Metaverse creatively to encourage outside interests—I'll say more on this later when discussing community and well-being within the Metaverse.

The Metaverse has the capacity to serve dictatorial employers to the fullest extent of their abrasive management approaches. If a manager exhibits an extreme lack of trust in their subordinates, there is an opportunity to encourage and coach that manager into a more temperate, empowering style. But as Metaverse employees become enabled through developing their technological skills, and as more companies transition into a virtual model, there will be no need for extremes in supervision because top talent will have their choice of where to work and will be sought after by companies who are in alignment with their professional values and vision. You will have the right people in the right place, and accountability will be a natural consequence of that rather than a set of strictures imposed upon your team.

The bottom line is working for and with people who are aligned with your own professional values. Employees who are nervous about the far-reaching potential of accountability in the Metaverse are demonstrating an appropriate recognition of the boundaries that must be established. This concern is actually profound, because it's a gateway to conversations about ethics that need to be happening around work policies in a virtual space. **In a healthy professional environment, privacy and accountability are compatible concepts that can exist together.** Striking that balance is the responsibility of every business leader.

The Erosion of Norms

Of greater concern is the erosion of norms that make bad behavior more likely in a virtual workplace than within four physical office walls. *Online disinhibition* is a phenomenon that occurs when people are less inhibited or restrained while engaged in online activities compared to real-life interactions. People often feel emboldened to express themselves more freely and act out in ways they would not normally do in a face-to-face setting. This misbehavior can manifest in the form of offensive or hurtful comments, cyberbullying, and online harassment. We've all heard the stories of egregious behavior in online gaming environments. It remains an urgent issue to be solved.

The disinhibition effect is a double-edged sword. Sometimes people share very personal things about themselves or show unusual acts of kindness and generosity. However, the disinhibition effect is not always so benign. Out tumble harsh criticisms, anger, hatred, obscenities, even threats. According to an undercover researcher at *New York Times* who was working on a report about sexual abuse and harassment within online gaming, a user who sexually abused her avatar commented, "I don't know what to tell you. It's the Metaverse—I will do what I want."

Sexual harassment in the workplace was a reality long before remote work, or even the anonymity of the internet, entered the scene. It can include requests for sexual favors, verbal harassment of a sexual nature, and offensive remarks about a person's gender. Many forms of it don't require the perpetrator and the victim to be in the same room or even the same zip code.

This type of harassment can and undoubtedly does happen in the Metaverse, as certain individuals will carry out heinous acts in every reality. And we do not believe it is any more tolerable or less violating if it happens in the virtual space.

Protocols around harassment need to be strict, binary, and razor-sharp. Obviously, corporations never want to become one that fails to protect employees of every race, gender, and sexual orientation from unwanted sexual advances, discrimination, or hatred in the workspace. More than one decade of experience has taught us the raw dangers of the cyberworld. The space very much is the Wild West—still largely uncharted and unpoliced. Researchers for the Center for Countering Digital Hate (CCDH) recently posed as minors, spending hours on Oculus and VRChat within Meta Platforms's Metaverse. They found that users were exposed to abusive behavior every seven minutes, including bullying, presentation of graphic sexual content, racism, and threats of violence.[3] **Hope for the best, but understand the likelihood of bad actors in the digital age, and as a result, expect and prepare for the worst.**

Employees whose behaviors are misaligned with company values need to be dealt with swiftly and decisively and without any compromise to the integrity of company culture. Sometimes the removal of a member of an organization is necessary. Cut your losses early to avoid greater problems down the road. Oftentimes leaders must conduct some uncomfortable meetings and have some exhaustive conversations, and in my early days working in the Metaverse, my colleagues and I had to traverse the digital terrain with no defined parameters of protection. The "law of the land" quickly becomes intuitive because the longer employees inhabit their digital bodies, the more connected they feel to their avatar existence. After a short period of acclimation within the Metaverse environment, users begin to make some of the same social gestures that they use in real life and engage in some of the same activities, such as standing up from your avatar's chair when another avatar introduces themselves, or waving, or dancing the samba, or driving a speedboat. Your avatar, in short order, becomes recognizable to other avatars and identifiable to those avatars who previously had only met you in person. Therefore, businesses must have policies and procedures around behaviors most internet-dependent companies haven't yet considered. As leaders of organizations, we need to protect our simulated communities with the same dedication we would demonstrate in a physical workspace.

Our avatars, these digitized versions of us, are very much us. And within the unwritten "creed" of our work world, it is understood that *we exist here, we do business in this space.* Therefore, harmful behavior is as violating as if someone were to harm one of our workers "in real life." And this complicates matters. Because while we can control and monitor the physical behaviors of our employees (making sure they are following protocol and holding them to high standards of interpersonal relating), we have to find new ways and tools to offer control over and protection from virtual violations like traumatization or being shown lewd sexual images by bad actors; being predated by those with abusive or hostile intentions; or having our employees' personal or professional information phished.

The apprehension around accountability in a virtual workplace is understandable. It is an entirely human response. From the perspective of the employer, not encountering their employees on a personal level—in the sense of meeting them face-to-face, either at the hiring stage or after their engagement—creates trepidation around embracing simulated campuses and avatar teams. For anyone who has managed medium to large groups in an on-site establishment, this trepidation makes sense. Depending on the nature of the work, quantifying and facilitating the productivity of a cohort of people can be challenging, even if their desks sit ten feet from yours. Combine this process with multiple campuses in a virtual reality, and this would create uncertainty for any conventional business owner or leader.

Virgin Group founder Richard Branson was an early champion of remote work. In his eyes, the success of a dispersed working model hinges on one thing: trust. On his blog, he remarks, "Flexible working is smart working. Screw business as usual. If you trust your people to make their own decisions, they will reward you."[4] And in another post, "To successfully work with other people, you have to trust each other. A big part of this is trusting people to get their work done wherever they are, without supervision. It is the art of delegation, which has served Virgin and many other companies well over the years."[5]

Chris Hoffman from the IT Collective also considers accountability to be rooted in trust, saying, "If we're struggling with trust issues, it means we made a poor hiring decision. . . . It's as simple as that. We employ team members who are skilled professionals, capable of . . . making a valuable contribution to the organization."[6] **Physical proximity is not the issue; trust is.**

Trust is an "evolving thing that ebbs and flows," says David DeSteno, a professor of psychology at Northeastern University and the author of *The Truth About Trust*. Trust is built slowly through repeated interactions that take place over a long period of time. The kind of trust that engenders accountability in a virtual workplace has a 360-degree quality: leaders trust team members, team members trust leaders *and* each other, the leadership team shares a mutual sense of trust and respect. Outside stakeholders are also part of the trust circle, be they clients, suppliers, partners, or vendors.

Business leaders can take six actions/stances to foster trust in the Metaverse.

1. **Make a connection:** Get to know the people on your team and let them get to know you. Walk the hallways in the Metaverse and have conversations along the way: find out someone's favorite football team, ask about the family photo on the walls in their Metaverse office, share stories about your respective hometowns. When you emphasize common ground, employees believe your goals are aligned with theirs.

2. **Be transparent and truthful:** Share as much as you can about the current health and future goals of your organization. If you fail to tell people about the hard stuff as well as the happy news, they won't see a reason to trust you.

3. **Encourage rather than command:** Motivating employees to succeed on their own will earn their trust. Grant as much autonomy as you can while laying out your expectations clearly.

4. **Take blame, but give praise:** No one appreciates a boss who basks in all the glory of success but rushes to point the finger when things don't go their way. Instead of casting blame on your team for layoffs or poor profits, admit mistakes. Stress that it is the organization—and your own leadership—that has work to do.

5. **Say no to favoritism:** If you treat some people better than others, their belief in you will crumble. The Metaverse is a great environment for including everyone equally; there's no limit to how many people can fit in a virtual meeting, so make sure the doors are open to all.

6. **Be competent:** Even a well-liked leader has to be good at what they do in order to be trusted by the team. Update your skills regularly; follow through on the commitments you make. And never fake it until you make it—employees will respect you far more if you acknowledge what you don't (yet) know.

Leaders Set the Tone

In any discussion of workplace accountability, focus needs to be directed at top-down accountability. This goes hand in hand with transparency, which we considered in chapter 3.

Good leaders want to be held responsible for their actions. The beauty of the Metaverse is its ability to accurately track and share *our* progress, too. Nothing creates more transparency and trust than regular meetings with the teams to discuss leadership's successes and shortcomings. With its many tools for accountability tracking, the Metaverse can provide the necessary data to create a common goal among supervisors and their teams. Once roles are established and expectations are set, both leaders and employees can be positioned to succeed in a way that complements the other. The Metaverse can be utilized as a device that encourages, educates, and develops every professional with a desire to grow.

Governance is needed in the Metaverse in order to achieve the goal of all team members being safe within it and ensuring that accountabilities, decision-making rights, and incentives guiding behavior are in place. A rigor must be established, for instance, in conducting compliance training every quarter, and refreshing team awareness of topics such as phishing scams, malware threats, and sexual harassment. Make yourself and your organization less susceptible to these kinds of issues as a result of that rigor, which is necessary regardless of whether your workplace is brick-and-mortar or virtual.

Additionally, the assumption that traditional workplaces give you "eyes" on your employees is entirely false. Real estate agents, IT consultants, sales representatives—they all may have to be on the road a large part of their working day. In a real estate brokerage, you might not see an individual agent for months at a time, so your visibility is limited indeed. **In situations like these, trust is far more effective in establishing accountability than petty tyranny could ever be.**

A healthy Metaverse workplace requires adequate governance and the upholding of "Metaversal laws." We have learned from the internet's shortcomings in protecting our data and ourselves and must apply those lessons as we transition to the Metaverse, where even greater vigilance will be necessary due to its immersive, tactile nature. Ultimately, the success of the Metaverse as a work environment will depend on our ability to ensure a safe and secure environment for all who enter it.

IN BRIEF

The notion that you need to be in physical proximity to someone in order to hold them accountable has been proven not to be the case. As Richard Branson puts it, "To successfully work with other people, you have to trust each other. A big part of this is trusting people to get their work done wherever they are, without supervision."[7]

Image courtesy of Virbela

6

ACHIEVING PEAK PRODUCTIVITY

Purpose Drives Output

My first true job out of college was with the Massachusetts Office of the Attorney General. I was applying for a role as an assistant to a bureau chief in a satellite location of the sprawling agency. At one point during a series of interviews with different people over the course of several months, I was invited to meet with the Attorney General himself. As he entered his large office on the twentieth floor of the building, I stood to greet him as he made his way to his desk. I sat across from him, with the gold dome of the Massachusetts State House and the Boston skyline visible to my left through a wall of floor-to-ceiling windows. I could hear car horns sounding from the congested traffic below.

The Attorney General turned to me and asked, "Do you know your way around Boston?"

"Not at all." I replied. "I don't have any experience driving in the city."

The meeting concluded and within hours, despite my answer, I was offered the position as the driver for the Attorney General, who was also just beginning his run to become the Democratic Party nominee for governor of Massachusetts. I met influential people, and I was able to see briefly behind the scenes of (at the time) one of the largest political scandals in American history. It was 1997, and all the talk was about President Bill Clinton and the Monica Lewinsky scandal. Within a day or two of the story breaking, Clinton came to Boston to endorse the AG.

I worked sixteen-hour days, but every day felt like a field trip more than work. Each day was different, I was on the go all the time, and the work suited me down to the ground.

It all came to a crashing end when the AG lost the general election in the fall of 1998. I had been so emotionally invested in my work, I needed to find something else to throw myself into. At the time, I was dating someone who was taking the LSAT. Law seemed like it might be that next goal for me.

Shortly after, I was accepted to Boston College Law School. About four days into the first semester, when I had already paid half the tuition, I was sitting at my desk, which was loaded with a stack of books so tall I couldn't see over them. I knew I didn't want to read all this stuff and that I had made a terrible mistake.

While law was never an enjoyable pursuit for me, it did turn out that the skills and ways of thinking stood me in good stead and ultimately contributed to me being where I am today. But those early days were a slog. I came to see the corrosive effect of billing by the hour. I like to get things done—fast—so telling someone like me to bill in six-minute increments offered no incentive. When I shared my frustration with one of my colleagues, he explained to me how to work the system. "Here's one way you can do it, Jason. When you get to the end of the day, if you've been here ten hours and you look at your time sheet and you've only billed four, just take the remaining six hours and divide it among your clients."

"You've got to be kidding me," I thought.

I wanted out badly. In my lunch hour I would grab a racquet-ball and short-hop it against the wall and catch it. I'd do loops around the building, throwing that ball and catching it, trying and failing to imagine that this would be my life. When I was a teenager, I worked for a couple summers as a postal carrier in Lawrence. It was by no means a cushy job—I was chased off by dogs more times than I can tell you. Every morning I'd go to the post office and the rack would be full of mail to deliver. I'd go out, do my rounds, and the next morning the rack would be full again. The work was like a recurring nightmare; I never felt like I got anywhere. Law felt like that to me.

To my mind, I achieved very little of significance throughout those years. I wanted to be part of a workplace that was energetic, progressive, and productive (though the silhouette of what that could be remained unclear). My firm was by no means a bad one, but it operated the way many workplaces do—fueled by problems and negative reinforcement. The only time anyone would call me was when they had an issue. Then, they'd want to get off the phone as quickly as possible because I was billing in six-minute increments—and it was costing them.

During the ninety-minute drive to and from the office every day, I would be plagued by a work model that I knew didn't serve me. I could leave at one o'clock in the afternoon, I could leave at four o'clock—and I'd still hit Boston traffic. Our kids were young at this time; we had a two-year-old and a newborn. I never met my own dad, so it meant a great deal to me to be a part of my kids' lives. But more often than not, I reached home around their bedtime, snatching a few brief minutes with them at best. Days would go by when I didn't see them at all. "This is no way to live," I'd think.

All this time, my circumstances were pointing me toward a business model I didn't even know was possible. But all I could recognize at the time was that the traditional working model was unsustainable at best. While frozen between point A and point B on the interstate every day, I began contemplating new ways of making my living. Back then, the conventional work model was the only way of life most of us knew. It was near impossible to consider what (if any) jobs offered any flexibility or mobility. I felt like I was beating my head against a wall.

This internal conflict inspired my curiosity about remote work for its flexibility alone. As a remote worker, I could control my schedule—and to an extent my environment. I knew some people even had home offices, which seemed appealing yet odd at the time. I imagined what it would look like to create an office in my own home, with no time sheet in sight, and the idea felt empowering.

Once I took the full leap into eXp (and made it past the

difficult years of helping get the company off the ground), I learned that I was right. The Metaverse proved that the work environment I'd been longing for could exist. And that it was my purpose to actualize virtual business models in the service sector.

Though unconventional in the early 2000s, now the Metaverse is increasingly acknowledged as the way of the future. The Metaverse enables service-industry professionals to experience the luxury of its limitless functions while having their work life optimized. Employers have something to be enthusiastic about because they can now offer a work model that equally incentivizes and challenges their employees toward peak productivity numbers. The trackability of every function makes it possible to pay employees based on their accomplishments versus their agreement to simply sit behind a desk for eight hours a day.

As a result, I've seen global teams of quality workers fill every trackable work hour with purpose, passion, and intention. Because, like my younger self, they understand that time is a valuable resource—and they don't want to waste a second of it.

Here in Body but Not in Mind

According to a Gallup study, more than 50 percent of the Western workforce in 2022 engaged in a behavior called *quiet quitting*. This term grew in currency during the coronavirus pandemic when traditional workspaces struggled to go remote. The term circulated across social media platforms and was popularized by trending articles and comedic memes. It accrued some subtly different meanings. For some, quiet quitting meant fulfilling the on-paper requirements of your job, and they argued that there is nothing wrong with that (except in a workplace ruled by over-achievers). Here, I mean it in the sense of mentally checking out from work, becoming detached but not formally quitting. Workspaces that were not prepared to transition from an on-site establishment to a remote model faced the frustrating reality that in the comfort of their own home, many workers put in less effort. Managers took note when employee statuses would default to "Away" for long periods of time, this indicating that they might be snatching extra breaks, turning on the television, sleeping, or taking prolonged lunch periods.

While none of this behavior is excusable, much of this could have been prevented had these companies at least had a template of what it would mean for their organization to go remote. Having the benefit of leading virtual teams for a decade by that time, I was frustrated to see that so many organizations were failing to execute an effective virtual strategy.

After up to eighteen mentally taxing months indoors, employers across the globe started inviting their workers back into the office (at least part time). By 2023 many big employers were becoming impatient with workers' attachment to remote or hybrid work models. At the World Economic Forum in Davos, Morgan Stanley CEO James Gorman didn't hold back about his thoughts on the flexible work culture, declaring that working remotely is "not an employee choice." He went on, "They don't get to choose their compensation. They don't get to choose their promotion. They don't get to choose to stay home five days a week. I want them with other employees at least three or four days."[1]

Remember that at the time James Gorman made this statement, the pandemic was far from over. As a result of the combined stressors, employees became ambivalent and their productivity declined. They began to contribute the bare minimum at work—just enough to hit their targets, before quietly fading out the rest of the day; some defaulted to beefing up their resumes on the clock—or looking on job hubs for employment elsewhere. All because of work fatigue in an environment where there was no correlation between productivity and purpose—the latter of which people desired more than ever after experiencing a traumatic, isolating historic event.

I maintain that regardless of global tragedy, if employees are removed from their purpose under the umbrella of an organization, the overall work model is flawed. Because the Metaverse bridges the gap of disadvantages and empowers workers to exceed their greatest professional goals, I've seen team members blow past the objectives they initially aim to accomplish. This is what happens when organizations from day one set them up for success.

I have deliberately set out to dismantle any preconceived notions about the remote work environment being isolated, stale, or unstable. In every way, a Metaverse-based model can align with an employee's goals—ultimately motivating them to keep their productivity up while they are on the clock. I see this in virtual gatherings: the natural momentum generated by having a team full of avatars waiting for a fellow employee to join the digital luau, climb aboard a virtual pontoon, join in the campus meeting room, or take a field trip to a nearby park. The Metaverse requires a level of engagement that tools such as

Zoom and Slack do not. I see this as being the opposite of *digital presenteeism*, the label that virtual workplace consultant Larry English applies to the pressure to be "seen" online at certain hours of the day that remote or hybrid workers experience. They may also feel pressure to respond instantly to chats or emails, or offer comments on documents simply as proof of work.[2] Yet visibility does not equal results. "Instead of number of hours worked, meetings attended, spreadsheets produced, and other meaningless metrics, leaders need to measure employees by outcomes, setting specific, measurable goals so people always know how they're performing," English argues. "They need to communicate to employees how they are doing on a regular basis, and not just during an annual review."[3] I couldn't agree more.

The intrinsic motivation to stay employed at an organization is largely dependent on whether an individual is appropriately placed, valued, and given appreciated work at a company. It has very little to do with their physical location and everything to do with the relationship between leaders and employees.

One practice I have found most effective in fighting the quiet quitting trend is inspiring employee collaboration. And the level of co-creating the Metaverse offers is unlike anything traditional workspaces have ever seen. While the temporary transition to remote work environments prompted by the pandemic was a step in the right direction, it still didn't solve the issue both conventional on-site and traditional remote workspaces face: a lack of outstanding collaboration options.

The Metaverse enables the industry's best to unite from all over the globe and share a virtual workspace. They can gather around a table or whiteboard, with all necessary tech supplies and the boundlessness of the Metaverse itself. The conversations that take place here spark even more than productivity. They go one step further and encourage employee *innovation*. No matter where an individual is positioned in the structure of the company, and no matter how long they have been with the company, everyone gets to participate.

No business-minded professional with a penchant for growth ever forfeits the opportunity to meet with avatar leadership teams because they are invaluable. Therein: people get paid to grow, thrive, and reach their fullest potential. And this is how a workspace should be. You don't have to worry about quiet quitting when your people are too aligned, too valued, and too much in your line of vision to quietly slip out the virtual back door.

More than good business principles driving this recognition is the wholehearted belief in what our employees have to share with us, and what we intend to offer them in return. Mutually, everyone has something worth banding together about; and as a result everyone has something worth staying for.

Activating as an Avatar

Brick-and-mortar offices are the perfect place for an employee to get distracted—especially when it comes to spaces driven by hourly billing. When we consider the reward system of the human brain, this makes sense. Workers finish a task, then receive a dopamine hit. But if they've clocked in at their traditional nine-to-five job, knowing that for the next eight hours they'll be wading through a sludge of time, they are less inclined to complete those tasks in a rapid manner. Why would they? If the expectation is merely seat warming, many other things can provide a reward chemical rush to the brain. Workers kill time at their desk, daydreaming as the bubbles in their Diet Coke cans rise to the surface. They are drawn by the omnipresent allure of internet surfing, TikTok, Candy Crush, and YouTube. When the imagining and distraction grow stale, they circle the watering hole (aka the watercooler or break room) and become completely immersed in chitchat about their colleagues' personal lives. Their intention may not be to steal time off the clock; but the more they settle into bad habits, the more "time theft" takes place.

In reality, this is the fault of the employer as much as it is of the employee. No professional wants to waste their life sitting at a desk where their work has little impact and zero incentive. As creatures of habit, they'll pass the hours being paid for grunt work that is done poorly (if at all). And everyone in this equation loses.

Working avatar-to-avatar is such a different experience. The Metaverse requires the use of many of our senses, activating the brain and keeping us focused. Because engagement and culture are (and have been) critical values in the organizations I have been a part of, I see the benefit in ensuring every person will be asked to give their input at least once in a meeting. Employees love this because it makes them feel valued, heard, and like they are contributing to the team. Most won't want to give up the opportunity to have their say, because they know that no matter how large the group is, they will have a moment where their thoughts are heard and their involvement is recognized.

In the Metaverse work environments I have been a part of, team members are rarely disengaged; the most we experience is a delay to unmute their mic. But we know they are there, because they'll be sitting with us at a virtual roundtable, nodding, blinking, shifting in their seat, eager to participate. And this attunement in the remote space never *stops* feeling profoundly more special than the traditional post-sugar-coma afternoon meeting in a fluorescent-lit boardroom.

Many have transitioned from traditional settings where they have felt less effective and also less valued. When they arrive in a Metaverse workplace, they finally feel productive, and they are surprised to experience more energy (and a higher rate of productivity) by getting more done. Some of this is also due to the redistribution of time. They don't have to wake up early, have their energy siphoned by traffic, feel adrenal fatigue by 9 a.m., then be plagued by pointless calls that could have been emails. They wake up, they have more quality time—to eat a healthy breakfast, take their dog for a walk, meditate, have a cup of coffee, and prepare for the day. They also have a clear understanding of when they will be expected to be "on" and provide input.

The best kinds of Metaverse meetings are infused with values, driven by clear objectives and highly specific goals. And in every meeting, participants can learn something new: industry methods look different across the globe, and team members are afforded the opportunity to have access to a worldwide range of professionals with whom they can converse, share, and collaborate.

As a case in point, the Joint Strike Fighter (JSF) program

is the largest fighter aircraft program in the world, with collaboration between eight countries: US, UK, Canada, Italy, Netherlands, Norway, Denmark, and Australia. This massive engineering project uses virtual workplaces to bring together engineers, designers, and other stakeholders from around the globe. The virtual workplaces allow teams to collaborate in real time, share designs and ideas, and track progress. The use of virtual workplaces has been crucial to the success of the JSF program. By bringing together experts from different countries, the program has been able to take advantage of the unique skills and knowledge of each team member, and leverage time differences between countries to accelerate progress.

Within a Metaverse environment, everyone is invited to participate on a level playing field. And with these relationships no longer being confined to a single geographic region, employees in every demographic can learn from the industry's best, take that information, and run with it.

Considering the value of these connections on a large scale is pivotal. Not only can the structure of Metaverse meetings be oriented to preserve the No. 1 resource business professionals have (time), they also enable the sharing of insider tips and bundled tricks of the trade that professionals might have to take several business courses or get certifications to learn. Not to mention the networking opportunities that could potentially shave months (or even years) off the process of advancing business relationships. Whether it's forging connections that might point toward new leads or an eager sales professional deciding to relocate after learning about some of the hottest markets in the country—there is limitless potential to scale business in the Metaverse, therein increasing the productivity and longevity of one's career. (We'll take a deeper look at that topic in chapter 11.)

While it seems as though the use of a digital space—full of bright colors, unique sounds, brilliant virtual backdrops, and distinctive avatars—would distract from productivity, it actually provides enough stimulus to engage employees' attention and keep it for measured periods of time. The beauty of this truth is that the time saved by not having to position oneself physically at a desk in a specific office is energy that can be spent giving an extra 20 percent throughout the day so one can deliver more potency and presence—enabling individuals to see their capabilities in a new light and set professional goals for themselves they have yet to imagine.

The endless possibilities presented by the Metaverse will free up employers to get creative about their business model, and invite employees to rise to a new level of innovative, creative potential most conventional workspaces have never seen.

The age of the avatar is upon us. As the Metaverse becomes a more mainstream way to experience the workplace, fearmongering will inevitably grow out of control. The most powerful position to take as an innovative leader is to embrace the "new" and get educated about how this new digital terrain can bolster the values of your organization. Over the past decade, I've learned that if business processes can be optimized by technology, then they *should* be optimized. If productivity is boosted through helping workers plug into their passions, then this should be one of the core objectives of an organization.

IN BRIEF

With the Metaverse, employers can now offer a work model that equally incentivizes and challenges their employees toward peak productivity numbers. The trackability of every function makes it possible to pay employees based on their accomplishments versus their agreement to simply sit behind a desk for eight hours a day.

Image courtesy of Virbela

7

A (VIRTUAL) LEVEL PLAYING FIELD

Dismantling the System

Though I was born in Boston, I grew up in Lawrence, Massachusetts—a city that, in the late seventies and early eighties, had a difficult time embracing an influx of immigrants from the Dominican Republic and of Spanish-speaking Americans, most notably from Puerto Rico. The largely Irish and Italian Catholic communities would use derogatory terms for Hispanic people. The racial intolerance in public places was palpable: sneering, name-calling, at times physical altercations.

Even my own relatives would defend racist banter by saying they were "just joking." But my mother did not like other people saying these things around me. Anytime I was in the room and somebody was denigrating people based on race, she would be proactive and speak her position so I would hear it. I don't think my mother has a racist bone in her body.

My mother believed it was Lawrence's aversion to the poor that kept the city economically impoverished. "That's what a resistance to growth and newcomers will do to a place," she'd say. She believed prejudice only yielded lack: lack of growth, lack of prosperity, lack of success, and lack of character. I didn't know it at the time, but I was watching my mother intently, absorbing her influence. I cannot help but believe it was her core values that shaped the way I would do business as an adult—and it certainly influenced me to dismantle the traditional way of doing things.

My business values derive in part from my childhood experiences. I grew up facing socioeconomic disadvantages firsthand. When I wasn't watching my single mother struggle to make ends meet, I was observing systemic inequality wreaking havoc on my community. To make matters more confusing, my experiences in Lawrence contrasted starkly with my days attending private school in Andover, populated by wealthy kids from one municipality over.

During the day, I experienced the privileges that a scholarship (and the hard work of my mother) afforded me. Still, life was strained in a different way. In the school pick-up line, everyone knew me because of my mother's bright yellow 1977 Chevy Nova with big rust spots. Nobody felt all that bad about pointing and smirking. That car was a symbol of the lack that seemed to follow me around, even through the doors of privilege. On one hand, I had so little compared to my peers at school; on the other, I had more than most compared to those in my neighborhood.

Seeing society from both sides enabled me to see the good and the bad in people regardless of their bank balance. I came to understand that I don't have a problem with people who have money—but I do have a problem with people who are entitled. I also don't have a problem with people who are impoverished, because I have seen how some groups are denied access to economic opportunity.

Now I am in the fortunate position of having some small measure of success, and one thing I believe to be a universal truth is that all people deserve to be unburdened from prejudice and given the opportunity to earn a reasonable wage. **That's why the Metaverse is so much more than a technology tool to me: it is a chance to change the world and influence how people fundamentally see themselves *and* others.** It is a chance to eradicate toxic social norms, call out aggressors, and encourage cultural conversation. As demonstrated in chapter 5, remote workspaces give everyone the same starting point, ultimately diffusing unhealthy power imbalances.

The Metaverse offers a more equitable, moral, and fair way of operating than the traditional brick-and-mortar model. Plus, healthy workplaces drive profit. Positive reinforcers, fair competition, feeling valued at work, and being paid according to one's contribution cultivate an environment where employees aim to have an impact—and where they are fairly hired, evaluated, and promoted.

The Removal of Optical Bias

Every employee brings intrinsic value to a workspace: their passion, purpose, motivators, and what keeps them energized and focused while on the job. In an ideal hiring process, these assets would be the determinants that get candidates hired. Still, in conventional workspaces, *optical bias* inexorably sways the judgment of hiring managers. Whether we like it or not—and whether it is fair or not—considerations such as appearance, aesthetics, and personal mannerisms affect the opinion of potential employers.

Though hiring teams are contractually prohibited against discrimination based upon race, religious background, political affiliation, sexual orientation, or gender, discrimination influences professional opinions all the time, as remaining impartial is difficult (if not impossible) when it comes to weighing business decisions.

Every choice we make is a representation of how and where we were raised, and what value system drives our lives. Therein, we see trends of inequality in professional environments across the globe—leaving marginalized groups underpaid, underemployed, and in the trenches of systemic oppression and socioeconomic disadvantage. The Metaverse is the solution to optical bias. In my professional experience I have seen it foster objectivity, inclusivity, and a celebration of diversity throughout an international community.

Bias is eliminated through practices such as blind interviews, where hiring teams meet with candidates without seeing their faces. After orchestras started using blind auditions, representation of female musicians in symphony orchestras increased from 5 percent to well into the 30s (and still rising).[1] It follows that interviewing as an avatar might diminish the effect of bias—unconscious or otherwise—against people on the basis of their gender, age, or appearance.

In a world populated by avatars, we are not limited by our physical forms to express ourselves (personally or professionally). We began as blockheads, and even though avatars have become remarkably lifelike, there are no rules around looking human, even for the work environment. You can express yourself however you like in avatar form. At OMNUS, the Metaverse campus has a wardrobe room where you can not only select clothing, but also your skin tone, hair volume and color, eye color, or religious headdress. If someone feels they are better represented by purple dreadlocks, rainbow eyes, or a neon green tie, no one's stopping them. This is one of the more fun, innovative aspects of using the Metaverse to dismantle preconceptions and focus on the assets each individual brings to the team. Making these options available to employees sends a powerful message: *come as you are.*

The Metaverse brings oxygen to our work environment, revitalizing the way we engage each other. No pressed khakis necessary for interviews; no suits and ties. Just me and my avatar—a neutral slate that gives employers a chance to evaluate the most important data about prospective hires: work history, portfolio, communication skills, accolades, commendations, and skill set.

This levels the playing field between candidates and employers and makes pairing with the best fit a more authentic, straightforward process. As a result, organizations and agencies see appropriately placed hires, increased retention rates, stronger productivity numbers, and more revenue overturn.

All parties walk away having participated in something more meaningful than simply bringing on a new hire—they've made an authentic connection, and leadership has truly *seen* the candidate for everything they have to offer, as opposed to only perceiving them through the distorted lens of a biased society, which rarely (if ever) showcases the raw skill set and talent of a dedicated business professional.

I would encourage any traditional workspace that values inclusivity to consider the following paradox: the inability to *see* an employee's physical features, clothing, and behaviors inevitably shifts an employer's attention to the more interesting and critical qualities candidates bring to a workplace. Meaning: the future is full of organizations that empower people of every race, nationality, gender, age, weight, height, and background to come as they are and offer their personal best—increasing a company's ability to become a "disruptor" in their industry by means of a healthier, more diversified work ethos.

I believe civil discourse is integral to *every* virtual community, that every opinion is valid, that every voice matters—that every person can be heard while communicating peacefully. It's been commonly said that the internet is the space where everyone puts on a mask, so "it's much easier to bully online." That's one opinion—but I think the way we remedy this is by infusing technology with intention. Yes, these are trackable platforms that will hold our digital footprint for the rest of our lives—so we should evaluate the impact we can make, and communicate accordingly.

What good is being a pioneer of the Metaverse if we aren't actively demonstrating how to use it for the good of humanity?

Paving the way for the future of technology means seeking ways to demonstrate the *positive* functions of a virtual reality. There have to be leaders setting examples on public discourse—especially when it comes to the conversation of equality.

When we speak about marginalized groups, we do so with the intention to lay a better foundation for the future of tech than we did with the World Wide Web. And progress is happening. In spring of 2022, the World Economic Forum came together with tech partners including Meta Platforms, Microsoft, and Sony to discuss what it will look like to create better protections for marginalized people groups in the Metaverse from bullying, harassment, and hate speech.

Untapped Ability

Karen Thomas came to work with eXp Realty in 2015. The southern-based broker arrived with a demonstrated history of success and compliance leadership in the industry. Karen was approachable, a trait that generally lends itself well to customer and client relations. She was a mastermind on the job and offered tremendous value to company character.

When Karen passed away, many of her colleagues were surprised to learn she'd had multiple sclerosis and worked every day from her wheelchair. While Karen had disclosed her condition (and the challenges that accompany it) to me several months earlier during a one-on-one Metaverse meeting, she never chose to disclose that information to anyone else at the company, and nobody at the company ever asked. Before coming to work in the Metaverse, Karen had faced a litany of setbacks due to ableism. In a perfect world, her medical condition wouldn't have limited her potential to do a great job and to get ahead professionally, which led leadership to question the value of this knowledge in the first place. What preconceived notions might be formed about a candidate by learning that they use a wheelchair? What subconscious biases do hiring managers hold that influence their perception of workers with disabilities?

If these factors cannot be detected in the way a candidate conducts themselves in a professional space, they should have no bearing on whether that person is hired for the job.

The Americans with Disabilities Act became law in 1990 to help remove barriers in the workplace and in daily life for people with disabilities. And yet inequity continues to exist. Data from the United States Bureau of Labor Statistics in 2021 shows that persons with disabilities were much less likely to be employed than those with no disabilities; 29 percent of workers with a disability were employed part time, compared with 16 percent for those with no disability; and employed persons with a disability were more likely to be self-employed than those with no disability.[2] At the very least, the statistics raise the possibility, if not the likelihood, that many of the part-time workers with disabilities would, given the option, choose to work full time. The barriers are real. And yet the pandemic created new opportunities for remote work that made employment more accessible to many. As *Fast Company* reported, when businesses were forced to recruit workers remotely, openings emerged for people who had traditionally been shut out of in-person jobs. As companies not only survived the transition to remote work but thrived, many of them finally seemed to have seen the value in better accommodating people with disabilities who needed to work from home.[3] They got to benefit from a wider hiring pool of earnest candidates, and previously disqualified professionals finally had a chance to demonstrate the breadth of their skills and knowledge.

This new framework provides a unique opportunity for companies to become leaders in their industry. I perceive it as a timely invitation for meaningful change. The cultural conversation on inclusivity is more relevant than ever, so embodying this value in an organization by employing the Metaverse is simply good business sense.

A True Open-Door Policy

The barriers to participation in the workplace are sometimes both literal and physical. In physical offices, geography can keep people separated. It's too easy to stay within your own zone: the desk or office you've been assigned within the area designated for your department. Even in a remote environment based on video meetings, siloing can be rigid. Video meetings are invitation-only, with little opportunity for breakout conversation and connection.

At the most basic level: if you're not on the invitation list, how do you get your voice heard? Without the right connections, how do you even know a meeting is scheduled? Can you engage with your organization's leadership team if they're based in another city (or even time zone) and you have no direct relationship with any of them?

Unless your business deliberately sets out to enable connection, the opportunities for interaction remain limited. With everyone in their own carefully delimited space, your workplace atmosphere can easily dry up and fall behind your competitors'.

Enter the Metaverse space, where, instead of being limited to a break room, people have the freedom to mingle in galleries, on rooftops, or out on the trails. With that kind of access, they can say hello, introduce themselves, explain their roles, and simply get to know each other—because they have access to each other in a way that would be difficult, if not impossible, in a traditional workspace.

Mitra Best, partner and technology impact leader at PwC, argues that this kind of access has significant real-world consequences for equality. Speaking at the Women in Tech panel at the Hands In 2022 Virbela user conference, she pointed out that, "Historically, women have not had equal access to promotions, high-profile accounts, or other privileges that come with recognition and reward. Virtual workplaces have the potential to offer us more access. . . . Simply by having more visibility into the organization, we have more opportunities to make new connections and showcase our work and our value."[4] Organizations also benefit from social equality, Best went on to say. "It's important to recognize that diversity actually leads to more innovative, more productive outcomes. . . . This is not just check the box. This is not just lip service. This is actually an important, significant, critical success factor for the future of work."[5]

Indeed, in my own assessment, the eXp community as

a whole is exponentially stronger as a result of its diversity—of religion, socieoeconomics, language, race, orientation, and identity, but also of professional experience. Real estate is one of those industries where most people come to it having done something else first. At eXp our agents were comprised in part of former cardiologists, engineers, schoolteachers, law enforcement officials, mothers, firefighters, technologists, fathers, marketers, environmentalists—you get the idea. And the diversity of these *professional* experiences when combined with rich personal diversity and that sense of ownership we spoke of earlier really generated a nearly unstoppable force of thousands lending their particular experience, expertise, or perspective in pursuit of building the best company we can because we all own it together.

Matters of the Mind

The term *neurodivergent* describes people whose brain chemistry differences affect how their brain works. They have unique challenges—and strengths. Possible differences include learning disabilities, medical disorders, and other conditions. Possible strengths include better recall, the ability to mentally picture three-dimensional (3-D) objects easily or solve complex mathematical calculations in their head, and many more. A sizeable portion of the world's population exhibits some form of neurodivergence, as much as 15–20 percent, according to a 2020 study. Business leaders would do well to attend to such a large slice of their current and future workforce.

For neurodivergent workers, morning routines are not as simple as waking up every day to a ritualized cup of coffee, putting on a suit that was selected and steamed the night before, and making a timely commute through traffic to take a seat at their desk. Things are not that easily compartmentalized. This is something I empathize with: in my teens I had some behavioral issues, and for a period of time my grades slipped as a result. Looking back, I suspect I had undiagnosed ADHD.

For neurodiverse employees with conditions including dyslexia, dyscalculia, speech disorders, and autism spectrum disorder, consistency is difficult. Larger assignments (usually marked by looming deadlines) create so much anxiety, neurodivergent folk have difficulty *starting*. If tasks are not broken up into bite-sized pieces, neurodivergent people are challenged by maintaining focus. Their planners are packed with sticky-note reminders, lists, and color-coded tabs. And yet, they often have a difficult time accomplishing the big goals they set out to do.

Should they manage to hold down a traditional job, most neurodivergent employees buckle beneath the weight of quarterly evaluations, continual disciplinary measures, or inaccurate judgments they absorb about their perceived character deficits. Though brilliant, they may fidget in meetings, stumble over their words, and feel perpetually underprepared. The traditional workplace also throws many sensory challenges in their path, with a cacophony of bright lights, distracting aromas, and constant noise. Much like those living with physical disabilities who experience the complex trauma of ableism, neurodivergents experience ostracism in conventional workspaces that do not set them up to thrive. This is a terrible business model and lost opportunity, because these individuals are often gifted with super strengths that would positively benefit a primarily neuro-typical organization.

Put someone highly creative with the capacity to hyper-focus in a coding chair, logo design role, or product development position, and they can refine a program or design to soar over the work of competitors. Unlike more methodical neurotypicals, neurodivergents have the unique ability to see things both from a high-level perspective *and* close up. They bring a transcendent level of detail, precision, and innovation to roles in an array of creative, educational, humanitarian, and technological industries.

Metaverse models offer a space for neurodivergent workers to come to the table, whereas in conventional workspaces they might find it profoundly difficult to even make it to the meeting on time. When inclusive environments are built for some of the most innovative minds (with the highest IQs), everyone wins.

Making space for mental wellness as part of the workday can include the implementation of programs, tools, and mindfulness exercises that support the brains of neurodivergent people by challenging their executive functioning skills and rewarding their brain with dopamine hits. Virbela's Mind Gym is one example of such a program. It is a specially developed community experience in the Metaverse, where those wanting to strengthen their time and task management skills can "exercise" their brains.

Neurotypicals rarely appreciate their advantages in small social engagements. Often, it's the little things that build rapport with coworkers: body language, social cues, inside jokes, intonation, and word choice. For neurodivergents who do not understand social cues, employees who speak with a stutter, or those with attention deficit issues whose words become "jumbled" when they communicate—interpersonal connection is difficult. For them, communication *is hard.* But having access to the Metaverse means it doesn't have to be. In a virtual environment, connecting is no longer reduced to verbal interactions. Employees can infuse conversation with everything from lively emojis to GIFs, if they want to leave an impression—*or* they are afforded the chance to simply respond more thoughtfully via email chains, team boards, and direct messages. Ironically, the use of technology can connect workers with their *voice* for the first time—an integral part of identity that some never experience in the span of their professional careers, and usually not in on-site business models.

Even beyond your neurodivergent team members, many other individuals may struggle to perform in a traditional work environment. If sensory overwhelm is an issue, for instance, remote work allows a person to control their environment rather than being controlled by it. "Async and remote in themselves are pretty life altering," says UK-based human resources specialist Yasmine Gray. "Not having to mask constantly, being able to drop out of meetings without losing the ability to contribute, being able to control the environment (heat, light, sitting positions) to help with sensory needs."[6]

Introverts, too, can thrive in the Metaverse. Lilac Ilan, former AVP ecosystem and innovation at AT&T, believes that a virtual work environment can allow for the empowerment of individuals. "The Metaverse tells individuals who may otherwise be stifled in a normal work environment that they can feel safe to share their views and be more vocal at the table. I think this is where the virtual world has a definite benefit compared to the real-world environment."[7] Certainly, I've seen firsthand how introverted team members can thrive when they can more easily share their ideas and views via avatar.

Joining the Conversation

An inclusive Metaverse is limited only by our imaginations. In April 2022, the world's first "metathon" took place. Hosted by deodorant company Degree in partnership with Decentraland (a 3-D virtual world browser-based platform), the event was designed to shape a more inclusive culture in the virtual world. The Degree Metathon covered 26.2 virtual miles of Decentraland's largest district, the Vegas City Sports Quarter, and incorporated accessible architecture like ramps for wheelchair users. By collaborating with experts in disability, race, and gender, the company incorporated a wide range of inclusive design elements into its participants' avatars. These features, which encompassed everything from wheelchairs to prostheses, running blades, and diverse body shapes and sizes, were accompanied by descriptive audio that catered to individuals with visual impairments.[8]

My hope is this: as society adapts to a new digital terrain, it will be one already built to accommodate those who have been historically left out—paving bright, equalized pathways for people of every nationality, race, gender, sexuality, and belief background to feel safe, represented, and empowered inside the Metaverse.

IN BRIEF

A Metaverse workplace gives everyone the same starting point, ultimately diffusing unhealthy power imbalances. My hope is this: as society adapts to a new digital terrain, it will be one already built to accommodate those who have been historically left out.

Image courtesy of Virbela

8

THE GLOBALIZED
EXPERIENCE

WHEN I WAS a junior in college, I spent one year studying abroad in London. It was an eye-opening experience for me to be exposed to such a different society. Having grown up in Lawrence, entrenched in a socioeconomic and cultural divide, with a mother who was intent on inclusivity and community service, I believed I was well-mannered and respectful to all. However, Londoners were unstinting in pointing out where I was wrong, making me see that I was far from the polite person I believed myself to be.

On my first day in the city, my flatmates and I were down by the River Thames when we asked for directions from a pushcart vendor. "Hey," I greeted him, about to launch into my question. To which the vendor responded, "My name is not 'Hey.'" From that moment forward, I began to pay closer attention to social interactions, carrying that lesson out of London and into my travels and business exchanges thereafter.

I didn't know it at the time, but that trip would be one of the formative experiences that prepared me to be an empathetic leader. It made me aware of how cloistered we can become, living and working in our little bubbles (and we all have them); and it made me receptive to the idea of diversity and globalization before I ever knew those concepts would be central to my career.

In the United States alone, we see a great deal of cultural diversity and political tension between regions. During the formative years of eXp, when I was working out the legalities of expanding to additional states, I took the time to observe the norms within each region—and how they translated across our digital platform. Each state had different regulations pertaining to physical office requirements, supervision of agents, and specifically the allowable distance in miles between a supervisor sitting in a physical office and any of the agents over which he or she has supervisory responsibility. I noted the expected differences between the North and South: northerners tended to be fast-paced and preferred direct communication; southerners enjoyed small talk and tended to be a little more leisurely in our meetings. Then there were the differences from coast to coast: Californians inclined toward innovative, creative, and at times eccentric approaches to work, whereas New Yorkers seemed focused on getting down to the bottom line of business. These varying perspectives brought tremendous value to the organization and the way it shaped its business model as it expanded globally.

As the company became "home" to more than 82,000 agents internationally, I recognized the unifying power of global virtual teams—especially in times of regional or international strife. Untouched by the perils of the pandemic, political and military warfare, and the physical ramifications of natural disaster, the virtual campus has provided a space for community members to gain perspective from colleagues of different nationalities, races, socioeconomic positions, and professional backgrounds.

This was especially true during the coronavirus pandemic, when America (alongside other nations) experienced tremendous racial, political, and economic division. Between conspiracy theories about COVID-19, dissension over mask mandates, and the disrupted mail-in election that was complicated by extremists on both sides of the aisle, it became impossible to have civil debates without confrontation or the dissolution of relationships. Every topic became politicized: Black versus White, the Right versus the Left, gay versus straight, Trump versus Biden. As much as I'd like to say we've progressed, three years have passed and we're still seeing the sociological ramifications of prolonged controversy.

Yet inside eXp's Metaverse campus, team members continue to learn from, share with, and support each other—even in the midst of a fiercely competitive market. The Metaverse affords the company the benefit of a safe, collaborative environment that embraces diversity and bridges the geographic, cultural, and digital divides between international employees—proving the effectiveness of the platform and benefitting the whole as it continues to pursue globalization.

The Benefit to Individuals

The beauty of the Metaverse is that employees are empowered to work where they want and live in places they traditionally couldn't. This has been true for Monica, a military wife who has been with eXp Realty as a staff member for more than eight years. The company's global model made it possible for her to build an entire career with accessibility to work that would otherwise be impossible for military spouses. Monica's husband is on rotation every twenty-four months to be stationed in different regions. Monica has lived everywhere, including Virginia, Tennessee, Texas, and South Korea. Thanks to the Metaverse, Monica has not only continued working with eXp, she has illuminated the particular needs of military spouses and families within our community. The Metaverse provides connection and practical support to employees in the midst of transition, or those who might be moving to a location of less access or little community.

One advantage of the Metaverse is that people no longer have to live in major cities to get excellent jobs. In 2022, a study by Upwork revealed that remote work has inspired up to twenty-two million Americans to migrate from high-priced cities like San Francisco and New York to more affordable areas of living. Almost 30 percent of workers surveyed stated they were moving up to four hours away from their original locations. This migration pattern among remote employees has increased by 3.2 percent since 2020, and this is just the beginning.[1]

As employers and workers begin to see the benefits of virtual workspaces (in the Metaverse specifically), the younger generation will be liberated to live lifestyles they've only dreamed of—whether it's millennials purchasing homes in more affordable markets or zoomers renovating vans to drive them cross-country. These opportunities will become available in mass proportion as the Western workforce embraces *working to live* versus *living to work.*

The Benefit to Organizations

At the start of the coronavirus pandemic, commerce depending on the purchase of physical goods stagnated, and online businesses boomed. Amazon workers were spread thin, overloaded with orders for survival materials: toilet paper, cleaning products, antibacterial gel, and nonperishable foods. The Western world also saw an increased demand for home-based entertainment services and items: streaming platforms, video games, VR headsets, books, toys, and so on. Anything to stay occupied amid extreme circumstances.

Shifting demands gave brands the unique opportunity to return to the drawing board of their organizations; they were invited to consider the versatility, scope, and span of their services. They invited their teams to contemplate what the "new normal" meant for their product line, whether it could transition to a virtual model, and how digital access would benefit their target audience. Businesses that were new to the Internet 2.0 were in a parallel space to the one I occupied in the early 2010s, just finding their way. Organizations that had functioned virtually for a long period of time were ready to cross the threshold into the Metaverse and explore the business opportunities of a global virtual marketplace.

According to Yogesh K. Dwivedi, professor of digital marketing and innovation at Swansea University in Wales, "Metaverse applications may offer brands the opportunity to extend their real-world positioning or to completely reposition their brands in a new environment."[2] He notes that Nike was one of the more prominent organizations that experimented with repositioning via the Metaverse during the pandemic, effectively creating a virtual replica of its global headquarters in Beaverton, Oregon, through a Roblox-powered virtual experience. Through their virtual campus, the brand could interact with potential and current customers regardless of location, providing virtual shoes, apparel, and accessories, and building brand equity using gamified events. Utilizing the functionality, fun, and versatility of the Metaverse, Nike was able to gauge consumer interest in the digital marketplace. They could entice their audience to explore this new way of connecting with their brand without needing to put even one staff member on a plane or ship a single box of gear out of Oregon.

The Internet 2.0 helped traditional businesses grasp the concept of a digital workspace; the Metaverse proved its dependability and its technological promise for the digital economy.

The Benefit to the Global Community

When I consider the globalization of eXp, I recognize that the success of the company in foreign markets will require a commitment to international community building. This has been made all the more evident in the post pandemic era. Despite the strange social fabric that's been woven amid the societal discord, eXp's team somehow became *more* interwoven as the world around them unraveled.

New team members joined the company eager to explore equalized opportunities, expand their networks, and become experts in the industry. All of them went on to benefit from being part of a diverse organization full of workers that had come from every industry: doctors, lawyers, salespeople, school-teachers, sanitation workers, call representatives, and more. All were invited to step into a personalized Metaverse work experience where they could collaborate professionally and bridge the gap between the physical and the digital through collective conversations on the pains of the pandemic and global discord. It was this structure that set up the community to grow in the same direction, despite its participants' differences being as stark as any.

The beauty of a remote and globally dispersed workspace is that it challenges international prejudice through exposure and education. What I've observed over the years is that America is a rather insular nation—a place where nationality, culture, race, religion, and dress create unnecessary tension and toxic dialogue. What I appreciate about the Metaverse is that it offers a space of neutrality, where we can slow down and explore these issues individually and collectively.

Every single day, I would see my US-based colleagues meet with team members from India, South Africa, Portugal, Brazil, Australia, or Mexico; they are exposed to societies that do business quite differently. Some, for example, require little or no explanation of orders and requests, preferring to make decisions quickly. Others expect much more justification about instructions and directions. The atmosphere in the room can be quite different, too: colleagues in the UK and Indonesia, say, are often more reserved and hide their emotions, while those in France and Italy may be more demonstrative. Over time, exposure to such differences leads to greater understanding and more responsibility—to be advocates for social equality, to disband biased opinions on the optimal ways of doing business, and to dismantle racism through the embrace of diversity in the workplace.

As individuals open themselves to a globalized experience, it is the responsibility of Metaverse-based businesses to support their international workers by navigating around potential obstacles that could leave employees from different regions polarized. They will need to strategize around time zones, connectivity, and issues of cultural disconnect so they can foster confidence in their diverse workforces as they expand beyond their geographical borders.

Bridging the Cultural Divide

For an organization to reap the benefits of a geographically distributed team, they must first acknowledge there is a downside to be dealt with—specifically what is known as "cultural discontinuity."

When a team of French researchers assessed the impact of cultural differences on global virtual teams (GVTs)—for better and for worse—they observed that "because of the diversity of perspectives within such teams, GVTs can have several advantages such as enhanced creativity, when compared to traditional co-located face-to-face teams. . . . However, despite the assumed benefits of creativity performance in GVTs, several boundaries or discontinuities such as time, geography, organizations, culture, work practices, and technology . . . need to be bridged."[3]

In short, and in my experience, the issues organizations face when attempting to globalize can be separated into two camps: practical and cultural. Practical issues can be addressed through planning and the exploration of progressing technology. Cultural issues require an entirely different type of proficiency, a human skill set that must be cultivated among leadership teams: the ability to use empathy, understanding, patience, and willingness to learn while integrating international employees.

A few years back, cross-cultural training solutions provider RW3 CultureWizard invited clients, end users, and business associates engaged in global business activity to participate in its fourth biennial global virtual teams survey. The survey attracted 1,372 respondents from eighty countries, in itself a demonstration of intense interest in this topic. After all, as the RW3 researchers observed, virtual teamwork is the basis of how global business is conducted today. "The survey points out how ubiquitous virtual teamwork is, and perhaps because of that, team members may fail to recognize the challenge of working with culturally diverse colleagues, especially in a virtual setting. No matter how sophisticated we become or how commonplace global virtual teams are, organizations will thrive and members will find it more rewarding the more people recognize that it takes special skills to fully capitalize on the enormous potential of global virtual interactions."[4]

What are these skills? When asked about the characteristics that made good virtual teammates, respondents indicated that the seven most important characteristics were the following:

- Being collaborative (19 percent),

- Being willing to share information (19 percent),

- Being proactively engaged (18 percent),

- Being organized (15 percent),

- Providing useful feedback (11 percent),

- Having good social skills (10 percent), and

- Offering assistance to teammates (8 percent).

The cultivation of these skills is important because RW3's survey demonstrates that almost 60 percent of international managers lack adequate training to integrate and lead GVTs. More shocking is the fact that more than 95 percent of these leaders were confident they *were* equipped to lead GVTs based on localized management experience. The study ultimately concluded that the only way to effectively lead integrated teams is to lean into what is referred to in the international business space as "cultural intelligence."[5]

According to the French researchers mentioned earlier, "CQ [Cultural intelligence] is malleable and therefore can be acquired by adequate training, interactions, and experiences . . . it is more than just the knowledge about different cultures. CQ is not specific to a particular culture and does not emphasize on mastering an individual culture, but it focuses on developing an overall repertoire of understanding, skills, and behaviors for making sense of the barrage of cultures that may be encountered in global work settings such as GVTs."[6]

To prepare teams for globalization, I have developed a simple three-point "Intercultural Playbook" to ensure they have trust in their leaders and feel recognized for their unique role, skill set, and contribution. The playbook is as follows:

1. DEVELOP LEADERS

The concept of *leadership* is interpreted differently across the globe. Some regions believe power should be tied to experience and longevity. Other societies deprioritize experience and focus on the executive functioning skills of a candidate: how easily and quickly can they make binary decisions? This is drastically different from the perspective of many Asian cultures, who value wisdom above all: thorough deliberation and taking ample time to lead well. Cultural intelligence in this regard means developing leaders who can strike a balance between all three of these qualities. While we can't please everyone, we *can* cultivate traits in selected leaders that are proportional to the needs of a team and not necessarily mutually exclusive despite their variance.

2. BUILD TRUST IN LEADERS

Distrust in leaders is one of the most prevalent reasons employees become destabilized and dissatisfied in an organization. This rings true even in a traditional setting. Add the complexity of a GVT, and a great deal of room is left for misunderstanding, miscommunication, and suspicion of authority—all resulting in an employee's declining desire to contribute to a team. Beyond developing leaders, the responsibility of an organization is to ensure managers provide an inclusive environment where they operate with integrity, empathy, and patience toward their team members. They must not only have clarity about their own intentions but also how each employee *perceives* their intentions. Managers should also continually seek to increase their cultural intelligence so they can effectively communicate with and mentor each professional they oversee.

3. INVITE COLLABORATION

Finally, employees across the globe feel valued when their opinions and contributions are heard. That said, many have worked in cultures or organizations where only the opinions of their superiors are taken into consideration. Out of respect to leadership, they reserve their own views for an appropriate time, place, and audience. Other employees come from open environments where participation is largely encouraged; they might not understand the more reserved nature of their colleagues. By engaging team members in a way that feels natural, universal, and inviting, they will begin to feel safe to share their thoughts and eager to collaborate.

Through the use of this three-point approach, leaders will be equipped to navigate the assembly of their GVT. As a result, the integration of diverse cultures will feel a little more seamless; even better, the team itself will bind together, creating a powerful dynamic that is entirely their own.

Bridging the Digital Divide

According to PwC's 2022 Metaverse Survey, more than 80 percent of businesses plan to integrate the Metaverse into their work model within three to five years. For many of those businesses, their primary goal is to move past localized borders.[7] However, PwC offers the view that the Metaverse cannot be a "force for good [without] underserved communities . . . those who need the Metaverse's benefits most [having access to the platform]."[8]

This lack of access among disadvantaged populations contributes to what business and technology journalist Charlie Fletcher refers to as the digital divide. With computers, cell phones, and high-speed internet needed for remote work, she defines the term this way: "When people do not have access to the technology they need, it creates a gap."[9]

The responsibility of remote organizations is to provide the technological gear or a work stipend that will cover digital necessities. Business owners must come to understand the specific needs of their employees and how that will correlate to their policies and budget as they globalize. Though the Metaverse is ready for the world, many disadvantaged regions still lack the infrastructure to support a remote work environment. Because

Western technology runs on progressing broadband connectivity, the United States is and will continue to be ahead of other nations when it comes to Metaverse access.

Economy acceleration expert Kieron Allen states, "The lack of infrastructure across all regions will enable richer economies to leap forward." He proposes that leveling the playing field for international Metaverse users will mean "creating technologies that are affordable."[10]

This sentiment introduces the revolutionary concept that companies creating programs and gear for the Metaverse have a distinct opportunity (even a responsibility) to revolutionize the industry by bridging the global socioeconomic divide.

Commenting on how this division is already visible, Charlie Fletcher adds that since basic computer skills are almost a necessity across all professional fields, a lack of access to technology results in a difficulty to find employment. According to Fletcher, "The FCC says that only 65 percent of people in the rural US have access to high-speed internet. Native American areas have less than 60 percent access. In total, nearly 30 million Americans don't have these services."[11]

She goes on to reference recent studies that demonstrate people of color experienced decreased access to necessary internet connectivity in professional and educational environments. Most made use of free workspaces including public and academic libraries for their places of work.

While such public resources do exist, the rollout of the Metaverse will present ample opportunities for technology companies to become more innovative and openhanded by extending 5G and 6G to areas of limited connectivity. **Only when individuals from every region, race, and culture can afford the same level of technological access will the full potential of the Metaverse be actualized.** This is where existing Metaverse organizations have leverage to promote equal global access. By their dedication to the equitable distribution of internet connection and hardware, global leaders can pave the way forward for equalized work opportunities in the Metaverse, and bolster professional possibilities for marginalized groups who have been systemically held back from advancing their careers.

When we talk about the potential of the Metaverse for corporate advancement, these matters cannot be divided from personal values and political positions. We get to decide the shape of the technological future now. I believe we are obligated not to repeat history and to provide ample opportunities for younger generations. Through these advances, we can use technology to facilitate racial equality and global tolerance, and change the lives of workers who have only ever known socioeconomic disadvantage, systemic oppression, and disqualification from any promise of lasting professional advantage. Then all of us will reap the benefits.

IN BRIEF

The geographically dispersed nature of a Metaverse workplace offers benefits to individuals, organizations, and the wider global community. It enables access to employment, scaling a business globally, and community building across borders.

Image courtesy of Virbela

9

BEYOND "BUILDING" CULTURE

UNLIKE CONVENTIONAL WORKSPACES—OR even remote environments with Internet 2.0—the Metaverse transcends "building culture" (by which I mean that based in a physical building) by bringing all manner of virtual possibility to the professional space. It suspends laws of time, space, and distance so employees can have a more satisfactory and efficient working experience. Things that would never be possible in a brick-and-mortar environment take place in the Metaverse all the time—from the practical (hello, speedy Help Desks and zero wait times on elevators) to the fanciful (I can actually dance well in the Metaverse). To clarify how waiting works in the Metaverse, an avatar might take a ticket from a ticketing machine (like at the deli counter). When their ticket is called, they are automatically ported to a team member's desk for the support they are seeking. The unlimited functions of the Metaverse are perhaps the most beneficial when it comes to culture-building. Not only does the platform's accessibility dismantle the notion that vicinity equals closeness, its versatility enables environments to function according to company values.

When culture is a cornerstone to an organization, a Metaverse environment proves that rapport can be built *beyond* the four walls of a brick-and-mortar space. Additionally, it validates the experiences of employees who have previously experienced conventional workspaces as dull, negative, and isolating. I count myself among them.

Practicing law in the early years of my career was one of the most solitary experiences of my life. After a cumbersome, frustration-filled morning commute, I would focus for up to sixteen hours in complete silence on transactional client work. With little genuine interaction, I felt my mental health waning by the hour. I looked forward to the occasional email or phone call to get me by. Then, when it was time to clock out, I'd make the exhausting drive home in rush-hour traffic.

By the time I walked through my front door, I'd ironically be so depleted from a lack of engagement that I didn't have the stamina to connect with my wife and kids. Naturally, this took an additional toll on my quality of life and tainted my job satisfaction. My entire life revolved around a five-foot-long desk stacked with papers and a hulking computer. I was miserable. I was lonely. And I wanted something *more*.

Though the state of my desk today in my home office doesn't look drastically different from my early years in law, my computer is now a technological window that ushers me into another world. For more than a decade, that world has daily evolved in aesthetic and scale. More than that, it has given me unlimited access to an extended family of team members across the globe who share the same values as me. In our Metaverse work model, I can honestly say I have *never* experienced professional isolation.

Individuals thrive when they feel included in global objectives, especially when they play their part in executing a common goal. These personal and collective wins strengthen the fiber of an organization and increase its long-term growth and profitability. **The potential of the Metaverse to reach and engage its employees is virtually limitless—literally.** The benefit of its adoption and thinking beyond a building-based culture generates an increased satisfaction and instilled sense of purpose that revolutionizes a workspace from the inside out.

Defining Culture within an Organization

In every business—small or large, brick-and-mortar or virtual, local or global—each employee has a role to play in culture-building. Typically, founders, CEOs, and company leaders carry the most influence in establishing, maintaining, and scaling this unified vision. This is why determining the collective understanding of "culture" early on within an organization is imperative; then the task is to define application steps to establish *how* this relational dynamic will be fostered. Ideally, the founders of a business can determine these matters in the first years of a company's inception—but I've learned they should do so not in isolation, but by inviting the perspective of their staff.

I define culture as *the shared set of organizational values and beliefs regarding how employees should interact and execute goals in a collaborative workspace.*

Early on in my career, I stubbornly held to the belief that the foundational values of a company are arrived at naturally, that they reveal themselves over time through the groundwork laid by the founders' successes and mistakes. I did not appreciate the importance of deliberately setting out to define and articulate what *culture* means to a company. Later, I came to acknowledge that my belief in values growing organically could hamper an organization's ability to fulfill its potential.

Back in the mid-2010s, eXp worked through a formal exercise of identifying, declaring, and memorializing its core values. For the first time ever, they invited the input of the entire staff. The organization hadn't yet expanded internationally beyond a few Canadian provinces, and it only had a head count of about five thousand agents who were geographically distributed across the United States. Wanting to pool the best information, the executive team considered quantifying employee feedback through sending out surveys—the kind of methodology you are limited to in a brick-and-mortar-dependent organization. However, after much deliberation, they decided to make the experience as organic and communal as possible. They blocked off an afternoon and reserved the main auditorium for those who wanted to join the forum. What ensued was a discussion that informed the pillars of the organization—a unifying list of professional principles they uphold to this day.

Gaining input in this manner demonstrated to me the importance of gauging employee perspectives, especially when it comes to matters of culture. And while the idea of working through a formal exercise at first seemed inauthentic to me, I learned that something revolutionary—and entirely real—could be born out of intentional connection.

Not only that, inviting everyone to talk about its culture helped the executive team to form a clearer understanding of the organization's needs. Because I was part of the team from effectively day one, I felt strongly that I already knew eXp's core values—and that we were doing just fine in upholding them. However, in seeing the impact of making employees feel valued and heard, I learned these principles should not be determined by senior executives alone.

Democratizing the Corporate Landscape

One of the greatest benefits of a Metaverse work environment is the democratization of our professional landscape. For too long, conventional work environments have been segregated into hierarchical categories and physical workspaces. In brick-and-mortar establishments, the higher-ups typically claim office spaces according to their position and seniority in an organization. Even more common is the incentivization these spaces offer during a promotion. Using physical workspaces to leverage "status" within a professional model that usually creates unnecessary dissension among cubicle employees. Because of this, it was eXp's aim during the construction of its Metaverse campus to entirely disband this model of working. Instead, they leaned into a lateralized, democratized workspace. Because the digital terrain is itself boundless, there was no purpose in siloing off business spaces for "management purposes." Wanting to preserve the values of inclusivity and accessibility, no part of the campus is "off-limits" to greener employees.

This approach, paired with an open-door policy, has facilitated years of openness and reciprocity between "seniors" and newcomers to the digital frontier. Because employees feel as though they can approach their supervisors with any idea or concern, fresh perspectives have been able to evolve the way eXp does business. Furthermore, it has solidified my opinion that executives should not be elevated among professional communities, nor should they be able to capitalize on being "untouchable."

In the Metaversal frontier, organizations can set a new standard. As expansive global entities embrace progressive technology, traditionally "competitive" work models will be flipped on their heads. Better paying and more ethical competitors will become the big fish of the digital ocean. Workers will no longer be forced—by lack of any other option—to take jobs that capitalize on socioeconomic disadvantage or insist on a specific geographical location.

Instead, boundless opportunity for the professional growth of every employee can be carved out along the vast horizon of the Metaverse. No longer will coworkers having "virtual lunch" with team leads be seen as a threat. Instead, these engagements will be commonplace and celebrated among avatar business professionals. They will represent equal opportunity for all—as opposed to lower-earning workers being pigeonholed into roles, tiers, and pay brackets that take advantage of their contributions and hinder their professional growth

Strategies for Culture-Building and Scaling

The coronavirus pandemic was one of the greatest challenges to management and leadership skills that I can imagine. Most traditional workspaces had no idea how to equip their teams for a hybrid professional environment or how to appropriately track their employees' digital activity. As a result, some used management tactics that were too heavy-handed, ultimately choking out the oxygen in their organizations. Employees who once enjoyed their conventional workspaces were left feeling suffocated by leadership teams who clearly didn't trust them so much after all. In response to being placed under strict supervision, these employees defaulted to doing the bare minimum required in their role while they sought other positions.

On the opposite end of this spectrum were leadership teams that were far *too* lax in regard to employee performance standards. In turn, they eroded company culture by losing once-efficient teams to the digital fray. Stagnating in confusion, burnout, and ambivalence, team members lost sight of company goals that once excited them and spurred them toward success.

Meanwhile, those of us who were practiced in establishing, maintaining, and scaling remote company cultures understood that the survival of transitioning organizations would depend upon creating a stable, digital atmosphere and equipping leadership to support remote teams.[1]

With the American workforce still in flux after several years of upheaval, it seems remote work is here to stay—to some extent. That said, as businesses progress technologically and shift to a Metaverse mindset, they can establish best practices that will preserve their company culture beyond a brick-and-mortar establishment.

Virbela, the virtual world platform (and part of eXp World Holdings, Inc.), has set out to help them do so by providing digital platforms for organizations to grow, and educational resources on scaling remote company culture. They identify three components that are especially effective for facilitating remote company culture:

1. Big meeting spaces,

2. Spaces to socialize, and

3. Prioritizing social events.[2]

Virbela offers a service that constructs virtual atmospheres based on the needs of each remote organization. Therefore, eXp has established the "heart" of its digital campus to be the main auditorium. This space has been essential to the integration of the company's workforce. It has enabled them to educate their staff and relay big news in a way that feels inclusive, communal, and thorough.

After long seminars, agents can enjoy recreational spaces that keep them engaged and entertained: digital sports centers, places to lounge, and walking trails to explore our campus. Additionally, there is the benefit of having comfy couches to recline on between meetings—and a cafeteria to enjoy a cup of virtual joe while talking to a friend.

While traditional business owners often argue "the workspace is not a place to be entertained," author Peter Miscovich believes the opposite is true.

The article "Flexible Workspaces Are the Future" highlights the work environment expert's emphasis on how "the office," as a construct, is changing. Because of "immersive" experiences offered by the Metaverse, "[Work is quickly becoming a place] to be entertained . . . to learn, to grow, to socialize." Miscovich concludes his thought with the idea that with increased technological advances comes increased responsibility. More than ever, pillars such as "socialization and team building and mentoring and learning [and cultivating] community" will be imperative as we migrate further into the digital work sphere.[3]

Taking the Roof Off the Organization

Even after many business owners decide to "go Meta" with their organizations, they fear the carefully nurtured culture within their brick-and-mortar facilities won't translate to the digital sphere. However, I argue the opposite is true. **By taking the roof off an organization, founders can scale a culture that desires to extend, heal, and grow.**

I include *heal* here because, after the cultural tensions presented during 2020, it is imperative that we acknowledge most international organizations are negatively impacted by socio-economic disadvantages and systematic oppression. The only way to generate new growth is to prepare organizations for full embrace of cultural diversity. We cannot speak about extending the reach of a business without understanding its cultural implications. Extending internationally means implementing global tolerance and integrating diverse perspectives.

IN BRIEF

A widespread fear exists that if you are not in the room with colleagues, there is no effective rapport. Yet the Metaverse is not like a Zoom-based (or phone-based) culture: many creative bonding experiences are possible that you could never offer in a physical office. With intent, a positive organizational culture is possible to build in the Metaverse.

Image courtesy of Virbela

10

REAL-LIFE CONNECTION IN A VIRTUAL WORLD

A New Kind of Celebration

In October 2015, Dave Gagnon, then eXp's head of growth, welcomed Traci Lewis into his virtual office. Traci was new to the Metaverse but understood the remote model to be unique and was curious about joining the organization. One meeting with Dave was all it took to persuade Traci of the benefits of "moving meta." Beyond limitless access to seasoned colleagues and mentors in other countries, Traci was excited about our global community that seemed very active in each other's lives.

Throughout the following weeks, months, and years, Traci stayed in touch with Dave via the occasional sidebar chat or office visit, or in person at company events, to ask questions, share tips, and strategize about how best to meet the needs of agents while growing the brokerage.

It was at one such event where Dave and Traci were able to spend a bit more time together in person. The two hit it off just as well in real life as they had in the Metaverse. As Floridians, they bonded over interests and hobbies central to their home state. Living close enough to visit each other gave Dave a chance to ask Traci on a date. By spring of 2019, they were in a committed relationship. A few months later, Dave asked Traci to be his wife.

We were happy to hear the news that two of our community members were happily engaged. When they made the announcement, I jokingly suggested they get married in the Metaverse so that we all could attend.

"We're actually planning on it," Traci responded; it took me a moment to realize she was serious. Their reasoning was that they wanted to invite people into the virtual world where their romance began.

For a while, the couple weren't sure whether they wanted to have a traditional wedding or a virtual one. They eventually landed on a hybrid wedding, something that could exist in the physical world while simultaneously being avatar-enacted in the Cloud. That way, they could invite as many of their international and out-of-state coworkers as they wanted.

When the coronavirus pandemic hit, Traci and Dave benefitted from their decision to have a hybrid ceremony, as there was zero need for travel and zero risk of spreading the virus to loved ones. Not only that, they were immune to disappointment because they had a great plan B. They knew if for some reason their physical wedding needed to be moved or canceled, they could always keep their virtual date. In good faith, they planned an in-person ceremony for September 2021 in Manchester, New Hampshire, and were ready to stream the service in the Metaverse—no matter the state of the world. Even though quarantine mandates had lifted by the time of the ceremony, the couple's guests still benefited from the digital wedding; their far-flung friends and colleagues were thrilled to attend a service they would have otherwise missed.

While searching for the perfect physical location and wedding dress, Traci and Dave also collaborated with Virbela to create an elaborate digital atmosphere where they could commemorate the big day. Drawing from the best of what they'd already experienced in the Metaverse, they wanted their virtual ceremony to be held at sunset, with a background of pristine beaches, open space for playing virtual games, and of course . . . a pirate ship anchored in the distance. Once the scene was set, the couple designed avatars that looked like themselves, with a gown and suit identical to their wedding attire. Before the ceremony, virtual guests were also invited to create avatars and dress in their finest digital clothing. Those who were unfamiliar with the Metaverse learned about the versatile functions of avatars—how they could talk, embrace, clap, and toast the happy couple. The Metaverse ceremony opened with my honor of walking Traci down the virtual aisle and concluded beneath the glistening lights of the digital dance floor, where Traci and Dave cheerfully celebrated with their guests into the early hours of the morning. Their physical wedding took place on the same day at the same time.

In both the virtual and physical worlds, an authentic and enduring bond was formed.

Catching up with friends Dave and Traci Gagnon
two months after their Metaverse wedding.

A Shift in Socialization

If there's one thing I've learned about the service sector, it's that most service-oriented people love being around others; they like social interaction, developing professional relationships, and connecting with mentors. They truly value building a unified team and striving for a common goal. And when they've had a rough day, they turn to their colleagues and share about their challenging circumstances.

This way of relating has always been a part of traditional workplaces, and it has been optimized—not erased—by the Metaverse via digital worlds made accessible to all. Instead of being limited to learning from or sharing with people who are in your physical office or perhaps zip code, you are instead learning from, sharing with, and collaborating with people/avatars across the globe. That isn't possible in the traditional office and isn't conducive to Zoom calls, where every meeting is scheduled and has a predetermined agenda. As a result, employees feel more committed to their places of work. In turn, they build lasting connections that refine them personally and professionally.

With the pandemic now in our rearview mirror, social interaction in the workforce has changed. As digital nomads have transitioned to remote and hybrid structures, employees have shifted their break room conversations to sidebar chats and Zoom calls. On Metaverse campuses, these functions are taken one step further in an environment where employees living countries away can connect and collaborate.

While the Internet 2.0 has evolved conference phone calls into video meetings, the Metaverse continues to provide more innovative ways to bridge the gap between distanced workers. The universal feedback from team members who are new to the Metaverse is how *real* engagement feels when they are on the digital campus collaborating with avatar colleagues.

The socialization experiences that traditional work models faced during 2020 was quite different. If there was one thing employees learned during quarantine, it was how to mute themselves during video calls. With the camera turned off and microphones silenced, workers mastered the dubious art of partial presence in remote meetings. The widespread social media critique of these calls emphasized how disengaging the medium of communication really was. While Zoom initially seemed ideal for unifying large groups, workers began to experience call fatigue and the meme, "That Zoom call could have been an email," was born.

Stacked against other Internet 2.0 programs, Zoom still reigns supreme in terms of keeping distanced employees connected when the situation demands. However, video-conferencing applications pale in comparison to a virtual world where mentors, colleagues, and friends are *always* present to each other (while ensuring clear work-life boundaries). If I see someone's avatar enter a particular room or suite of rooms, I might stand my avatar up, walk it over to the other person's avatar, and discuss our respective weekend plans. The use of avatars alone requires a level of engagement that activates users, rather than depleting their social energy or allowing their attention to drift during meetings.

Digital conference halls like eXp's main auditorium provide ample space for international employees to connect, share, and receive new information at the same time. After quarterly kick-off presentations or all-hands meetings, employees can assemble on the virtual quad for further conversation, or dance in the speakeasy to the selected songs of DJ Jazzy Jeff. Though traditional business owners might consider these moments to be superfluous or a waste of time, I believe they are integral to the well-being of a virtual global organization.

On-Campus Camaraderie

Paradoxically, a time of global quarantine offered a chance to prove that businesses can thrive virtually without compromising a solid sense of community.

There are plenty of people who, for an array of reasons, might feel uncomfortably exposed at an in-real-life company kickball game. In the Metaverse, on the other hand, no one has to worry about their athletic ability or how they look on the field. Participation by avatar takes away that awkward edge. People can jump into the fun without having to work up to positioning themselves (or being socially pressured) to *be* fun.

A thoughtfully designed Metaverse landscape of the future might include spaces such as shopping malls where employees can run errands during the day. Help Desks offer all manner of troubleshooting that employees might need. A commitment to providing excellent facilities for workers, even in their avatar form, leaves them feeling heard, valued, and seen. It also fosters connection between members of different departments and ensures employees' free time remains *free*.

Even better, many of us who work in the Metaverse say that when they "return home" at the end of each day, they truly feel like they have spent their time elsewhere. They consider the company's expansive virtual world a place where they can be entertained, make connections, and earn a living—even throughout one of the most physically isolating periods in recent history.

In an environment designed for global networking, employees experience more interaction, more engagement, more watercooler chats, more bonding, and more camaraderie than in most conventional workspaces. I know if I went on campus, at any given time there would be a couple hundred avatars there enjoying the facilities, some simply playing soccer or sitting by the water because they need a break. Not to mention the organic, innovative conversations taking place among our teams 24/7.

A well-constructed Metaverse campus is augmented by a lively intranet environment. Stakeholders in the eXp organization (staff and agents alike) can create private groups within the intranet based on countless shared interests and topics. You'll see members drawn together by neurodiversity, cooking and recipes, sports and entertainment, diversity and inclusion affinity groups, overseas listings they wish to market abroad, and so much more. In addition, the Metaverse campus itself supports these interests as well: with unity parades, competitive soccer matches between different countries (a Metaverse World Cup, if you will), concerts, and talent shows.

Image courtesy of Virbela

Whether through a birthday party, baby shower, break room chat, or meeting, the Metaverse creates room for innovation, sharing, personal expression, and comedic levels of unpredictability. I recall one such time during a meeting that accommodated more than four hundred avatars. For whatever reason, mid-meeting, one employee either thought it would be fun to start flying or discovered for the first time that his avatar could fly. Naturally, several others followed suit. Before long, the entire crowd levitated; we soared around the room conversing, laughing, and almost colliding into each other. For several weeks afterward, we incorporated flying into our weekly meetings . . . because crashing into coworkers in midair is a surefire way to remember who they are. By embracing the *play* offered by the Metaverse, I believe a company can be more professionally equipped and engaged.

This ease of connection has gotten our employees through difficult life seasons and sleepless nights—those times when we truly needed the satisfaction and camaraderie of kicking the digital soccer ball around with our colleagues in a different time zone. Because community never shuts down in the Metaverse, personal and professional support are only one login away. No matter how traditional some employees claim to be, this easy access to socialization is usually what warms them to the idea of a virtual workspace.

Such was the case with Rob, who was warm, endearing, humorous, and accomplished. He had become something of a legend at his former company and joined eXp in April of 2015. Rob was initially apprehensive about adopting a remote work model: He identified as "old school" and got a great deal of satisfaction from being present in a conventional office space. It took nearly six months of daily discussion, question and answer sessions, and some demonstration of competence (presumably) for Rob to feel comfortable making the leap (all of it immensely enjoyable and fun for me), but when he did it represented a tipping point for the company. In the middle of his early months with the brokerage, Rob and his wife, Kathryn, experienced the death of Kathryn's mother. Rob was open about the loss, the pain they were experiencing, and his need to attend the funeral in Ohio.

Upon Rob's return, he joined other avatars within his region for the weekly state meeting, all gathered on a rooftop of one of the campus skyscrapers. There, some thirty colleagues shared business insights, collective reports, and personal updates. Near the end of the meeting, Rob felt so moved to be back "around people" that he shared about his recent loss with the group. He acknowledged the pain he and his wife had experienced and admitted they could do with some support and even expressed that "my wife needs a hug." As Rob spoke so openly, every avatar on the rooftop got up from where they were sitting and surrounded him and Kathryn. They opened their arms and offered a large group virtual embrace. Today, Rob reflects on that moment and jokes that the culture he was apprehensive about was "eager to embrace him from the start."

During international divide and global uncertainty, I have seen the social fibers strengthened. When those across the world fell ill or died, we grieved. No avatar was left to face bleak circumstances alone. Throughout that time, we learned the value of a friend and that a single virtual embrace can be the one thing that keeps us moving forward.

As organizations continue to transition to remote models, opportunities for community building in virtual spaces will expand. **For community alone, business owners should consider becoming "early adopters" of the Metaverse.** Professional leaders who care about preserving community through the transition to a remote model should leap to learn the complexity, nuances, and offerings of the platform. As the next digital revolution nears, it only makes sense to abandon less effective ways of maintaining community and to pour resources into the boundless customizable options that make interactive campuses a feasible, long-term possibility in so many sectors and industries. The Metaverse has proven its effectiveness in sustaining distanced socialization; now it is the responsibility of business owners to infuse these possibilities into their evolving work models.

"Being Well" in the Metaverse

Perhaps the most enticing promise of the Metaverse is its ability to offer us unlimited virtual connection while preserving our privacy, autonomy, freedom, and professional growth. What I have learned over the past decade or more is that early adopters of the Metaverse commonly share the desire for their employees to "be well" in the workplace. As a result, diverse programs have been invented to promote a sense of community (especially during the pandemic), all of which encourage business leaders to transition their workspaces *past* Internet 2.0.

Pushpak Kypuram, founder of the virtual organization Next-Meet, succinctly argues for the Metaverse's capacity to connect people. "You can't keep twenty people engaged in the flat 2-D environment of a video call; some people don't like appearing on camera; you're not simulating a real-life scenario. That is why companies are turning to Metaverse-based platforms."[1] Like eXp, from the outset NextMeet was a virtual campus built for connection; and Kypuram's sentiment is correct—the opportunity to simulate real-life experiences has been one of the key drivers in remote businesses transitioning to the Metaverse.

UK-based PixelMax designs Metaverse workspaces that revolve around employee access, connectivity, and personal comfort. Their foundational principles are communicated through the implementation of their three core "be well" strategies, all of which are highly effective and adaptable in remote workspaces.

1. Create Connective Experiences

In the Metaverse, opportunities for connective experiences are limitless, as avatars are constantly roaming the campus. Still, some people don't understand the value of actively engaging with faces they do not recognize, or cold-prompting colleagues with thoughtful questions. To help these employees along, we have designed interactive information desks and posts throughout our campus to spur employee connection. A simple "Traci, have you met Dave?" can change the entire course of someone's career and life. Additionally, we host seminars in the main auditorium that serve solely as community icebreakers. While these events can feel inauthentic at first, we've found that they prompt an engaged environment where no avatar can stay insular for too long.

2. Establish Well-Being Spaces

No two Metaverse campuses look alike, and their offerings are individually designed. Depending on employee demographic and interest, the well-being spaces on a campus can be drastically different. Some companies might offer on-site art museums, movie theaters, or video game arcades; others might have wellness spaces dedicated to mindfulness-based exercise such as yoga, Pilates, or meditation. When workers have a space to connect, play, debrief, and rest, they are more likely to experience a sense of value in the workplace, and be more efficient with their time when they are actively on the clock.

3. Collaborate with Delivery Services

For those who haven't experienced the Metaverse, it seems unreal to consider virtual streets lined with shops that ship items directly to users' homes. But Metaverse shopping is really no different than buying from Amazon or Instacart. Just like employees in remote work environments can open a tab and have a pizza or groceries delivered to their house, so too can avatars stand in line, place an order, then have it shipped to a physical location. This means endless possibilities for various lines of business to transition to the Metaverse and for existing campuses to partner with them. Imagine the ease of running by the campus ATM to cash a check—no need to drive to a physical ATM, or even to open a banking app on your phone. Or consider the possibility of virtual bookstores; employees could browse titles on their lunch breaks and have a physical copy in their hands within hours (an eBook or audiobook within seconds). When we think about the fact that certain restaurant chains already exist in brick-and-mortar corporate cafeterias, or that coffee shops are built into the community centers of large healthcare campuses, none of this is too far-fetched. Need a caffeine boost before your last meeting of the day? Have your avatar stop by your favorite coffee shop and place an order. It's entirely reasonable to expect Metaverse businesses of the future to offer these incredibly convenient services that enhance a sense of well-being among remote employees.

If I've learned anything in the past decade or more, it's that as the Metaverse evolves, employees continue to shift the way they orient to their work environments. Where previous generations clocked into traditional settings to slog through monotonous tasks, the Metaverse offers dynamic engagement and a great deal of freedom—without jeopardizing productivity, as we saw in chapter 2. In fact, the platform demonstrates a positive correlation between entertainment and productivity—something that will fundamentally change the way Westerners, and ultimately the world, does "work." And this will likely appeal to different generations for a variety of reasons.

For example, boomers and Gen Xers tend to value the structure offered by conventional workspaces, while millennials and zoomers more often value fun, versatility, and autonomy.

Metaverse work models have the opportunity to offer both. The key is to make sure that these platforms are supported by the evolving technologies and programs that will keep them appealing to workers of all ages.

An efficient business in this space will protect the well-being of its "wiser" colleagues while maintaining a fresh approach for younger generations. Even better, they will create innovative ways to facilitate community between older and younger age groups—underscoring the sentiment that *all* employees are integral to the well-being and lasting impact of a Metaverse organization.

Infinite Community

Community is infinite. This is something I remember every time one of my colleagues hosts a holiday party, talent show, trivia night, or virtual happy hour. In a Metaverse world, the moments that happen outside of working hours create some of the most impactful memories of our lives.

This is true even in brick-and-mortar establishments. We've all had the experience of an outstanding employee field trip, field day, or Christmas party. At the best of these events, everyone shows up as *more* of themselves; they are not drained by work stressors or the project in front of them, nor are they rushing off to their next meeting. They are simply present. This presence inspires organic connection among coworkers, and creates lasting relationships within an organization.

These relationships are why employees stay with a company.

And I maintain that, with a creatively designed Metaverse model, these experiences can be prompted and cultivated among a workforce, making its corporate character richer overall.

In an article for *Fast Company*, journalist Zara Stone details the "pre-game" monthly ritual of Janelle Barrera, a researcher at telehealth start-up Doxy.me. The piece begins with a depiction of how Barrera arranges her living room to ensure she has enough space for paintball in a VR hangout space with colleagues who are spread across the country—and have never met in person.

"Barrera ducks behind a boulder as she dodges a bullet, reloads, then pops up and fires. . . . for Barrera, the Metaverse is a place to unwind, to bond in a way that's more immersive than straightforward video calls. 'It's cool . . . it really keeps us engaged.'"[2]

You'll notice in Barrera's account of bonding with her coworkers, she doesn't have to see them in person to feel connected to them as a team member. The memories she's made with them, although virtual, have mileage. They are genuine and deeply felt. Anyone who has ever worked in a Metaverse model understands that when avatars move on, they are genuinely missed, as much as in any physical environment. No one leaves without a proper goodbye party and virtual cake. And I love to hear stories of employees who have chosen to remain connected in the physical world long after they have left campus. These stories show that the interconnectedness of community extends beyond our comprehension.

Like Traci and Dave, Metaverse colleagues can bring their virtual connection into a real-life interaction. One of my favorite stories that demonstrates the engaging nature of a Metaverse workforce is that of Stephen, an agent who joined us from the Pacific Northwest. Outside of work, Stephen was a talented musician who occasionally shared his gift with colleagues during quarterly music nights or global talent shows. (He was one of the founding members of the Metaverse-based eXpressions Band.)

During onboarding, he developed a friendship with Anna from our onboarding department. After only a few months of virtual communication, Stephen flew out to LA to perform a musical piece at Anna's daughter's wedding—the perfect demonstration that Metaverse relationships are powerful, expansive, and transforming.

I have a decade's worth of memories in this virtual space that have evolved the way I define a company's character. Along the way, I have identified the one feature about community that many traditional businesses get fundamentally wrong: they attribute the strength of their company's closeness to their employees' ability to sit at the same lunch table each day. **And yet the most effective avatar-based businesses continually demonstrate how work satisfaction has less to do with physical closeness and more to do with being mentally engaged, personally recognized, and professionally challenged.**

Metaverse workspaces are able to offer that which is infinite: infinite functions, infinite possibilities, infinite connection, infinite support—and infinite community, there to evolve with us wherever our professional lives may lead.

IN BRIEF

The Metaverse does not have to come at a cost to social and psychological well-being—to the contrary. In an environment designed for global networking, employees experience more interaction, more bonding, and more camaraderie than in most conventional workspaces.

Image courtesy of Virbela

11

A NEW TYPE OF EDUCATION

Get into the Game

Keeping an eye on future plays, the NBA has embraced virtual coaching in digital arenas, and in 2022, "Coach Nat" (NBA Augmented Telepresence) was introduced to the world.[1] With a voice uncannily similar to Shaquille O'Neal's, Coach Nat— an instructor bot who teaches users how to play basketball in the Metaverse—told attendees at the All-Star Tech Summit in Cleveland, Ohio, "My role is help coach, train, develop the next generation of NBA talent. I know all the best moves, and I'm untethered by one single dimension. I can even make a free throw."

NBA coaches had grasped how the Metaverse could serve as a bridge between worlds, offering the instructional advantage of being coached by the best in the industry—even at a distance. They marveled at the access opportunities: how international athletes could connect with their teammates, coaches, and trainers from the comfort of their personal gyms.

Now coaches and trainers can synthesize movements through the use of VR, watch players through video platforms, monitor fitness gains through detailed tracking, and create strategies that will take their team to the next level. Not only that, the Metaverse makes athletics accessible for rising players who would otherwise be disqualified due to limitations of one kind or another, such as a lack of financial resources, travel barriers, or limited access to practice gear.

The Metaverse offers a new educational landscape where users can be trained in anything, even the most tangible of trades, hobbies, and career tracks—including athletics. When an organization like the NBA demonstrates the value of bridging the physical world and the Metaverse, they prove others can do the same.

One of the primary reasons business owners, educators, coaches, and trainers hesitate about adopting the Metaverse is because of its original orientation—gaming. "Isn't the Metaverse just for gaming?" leaders in every industry will ask. No—but it is the Metaverse's origins in gaming that make it a transcendent educational tool.

Education delivered through digital platforms involves users immersing themselves into a virtual world. Whether they incorporate Metaverse gear (usually earphones or headsets) or they simply enter their avatar design dashboard for a two-dimensional experience, there is a gradual sense of "becoming" digital. It is a personal "event." This virtual transition has been alarmingly "out there" for skeptics from the start—even me when I first discovered it. "Surely these gamelike elements will distract from the work that needs to be done here," I thought, clunky BlackBerry in hand. It wasn't until I embraced the Metaverse as a workplace format that I understood its educational power.

Indeed, the leading educators in the nation were among the early adopters of the Metaverse. While most universities were still navigating hybrid models, their progress accelerated by necessity during the pandemic, Stanford University created the Virtual People course—taught entirely in virtual reality. In class on any given day, students might float in space, gazing down on our planet; or swim among the vivid formations of a coral reef, observing in time-lapse style as the reef suffers the impact of ocean acidification and rising water temperature; or take a walk wearing a skin color different from their own, finding out firsthand what it is like to be on the receiving end of racial prejudice.[2] "To the best of my knowledge, nobody has networked hundreds of students via VR headsets for months at a time in the history of virtual reality, or even in the history of teaching. It's VR at an incredible scale," says Jeremy Bailenson, founding director of Stanford's Virtual Human Interaction Lab. The Virtual People course is built around learning by doing, Bailenson explains, "allowing students to experience and build applications that previous students could only read about, from therapeutic medicine to sports training to teaching empathy."[3]

Students find that virtual reality can provide a new type of education: one that appeals to emotional learning and synthesizing information through the lens of experiences. This revolutionary way of acquiring information promises to not only build knowledge but to shift paradigms. Arguably, the more abstract and philosophical use of these programs can help students build empathy, sympathy, and a sense of cultural unity in the physical world.

More and more universities are embracing the "metaversity" model. As part of an innovative collaboration, ten prominent universities and colleges across the United States have joined forces with Meta, the parent company of Facebook, and leading virtual reality enterprise VictoryXR, to create dynamic, 3-D "digital twins" of their respective campuses. These immersive virtual replicas are designed to update in real time as people and objects move through the physical spaces, providing a new way for students and educators alike to experience and engage with campus life.[4]

One metaversity builder, New Mexico State University, says it wants to offer degrees in which students can take all their classes in virtual reality, beginning in 2027. Though some students and teachers remain skeptical, wanting to uphold the traditional college experience, zoomers are a generation that has never experienced life without the internet, making them a primed audience for education, work, and commerce in the Metaverse.

The first thing that motivated Virbela founder Alex Howland to create his company was to develop an educational platform that tapped into the interactivity and presentation abilities of a virtual world. Alex came up with the idea when he was working on his degree in organizational psychology. Howland soon came to appreciate the effectiveness of leveraging an array of learning styles and capacities in the digital age.[5]

Despite our digital advances throughout the past decade, metabolizing the Metaverse is still a major leap for some training professionals. For those who are new to the platform entirely or who have trouble letting go of traditional learning modalities, a hybrid model might be the most suitable place to start.

The functions of the training platform, in this context, are not dissimilar from the remote structure many of us became familiar with during the COVID-19 crisis. Introducing it incrementally might include a video boardroom discussion using an even more lifelike camera display, offering a spatial, in-person experience that takes programs like Zoom one step further into the virtual learning sphere.

In my time in the Metaverse, I have discovered that the use of digital forums is an ideal educational format for most employees. Yet every industry, company, and professional will have a unique orientation to the use of the platform; it will be organic and ever-changing, and this "flux" makes it limitless.

That said, the Metaverse's vastness can be overwhelming at first. I have learned that it's helpful to find a common point of "teachability" among the most novice and the most technologically advanced employees. For us, that meant taking avatars and running with them. Laying that groundwork was palatable for those with little technology experience *and* those who were digitally orientated.

Remarkably, employees are continually learning and growing together in this space—as the platform evolves, the workforce evolves with it. As I write this, eXp's training teams conduct somewhere between fifty and one hundred hours of live Metaverse instruction every week. People facilitate those sessions from all over the world, with swathes of contributors in the UK, Australia, California, and elsewhere. Beyond accessibility and reach, the versatility of programs and how they can be replayed 24/7, 365 days a year makes the Metaverse invaluable for a global organization. Each instructor uses their own modalities, and the Metaverse offers a variety of mediums: think tanks, questionnaires, interactive documents, avatar presentations, and yes . . . games.

In my early career, I used to go to New York for continuing legal education seminars. In this post-pandemic time, exhaustive bouts of traveling for the purpose of training seem absurd; to expend the resources in order to sit in a room for almost a week seems irresponsible from a business perspective. Gradually, hybrid and Metaverse businesses are learning that employees can be just as easily tested and engaged from wherever they might be located. This means far more cost-effective and interactive opportunities for professional development.

Level Up Your Learning

The best advice I could give to traditional business owners is to *afford your teams the opportunity to have at least one virtual learning experience.* Even if it's only a bout of experimentation—I promise, the minds of even the most conventional workers will begin to change.

Training in the Metaverse offers saturated engagement through dynamic role-play via gamified learning technology; it is "learning via doing" in every regard. Players experience a spatial reality that appeals to all types of learners: auditory, visual, and kinesthetic as it shifts from telling, to showing, to doing.

Economics and technology advisor Mark Purdy believes that "the Metaverse could revolutionize training and skills development, drastically compressing the time needed to develop and acquire new skills. . . . In the Metaverse, every object—a training manual, machine, or product, for example—could be made to be interactive, providing 3-D displays and step-by-step 'how to' guides." He goes on to say that "virtual reality role-play exercises and simulations will become common, enabling worker avatars to learn in highly realistic, 'game play' scenarios, such as 'the high-pressure sales presentation,' 'the difficult client,' or 'a challenging employee conversation.'"[6] This template will be uniquely programmable among Metaverse learning spaces—making it an adaptable, appealing tool in every industry.

By way of example, Purdy mentions PixelMax, an organization we mentioned in a previous chapter that designs virtual reality campuses. They have teams working on games that "combine physical training with immersive gamification to enable first responders to do repeat training, try different strategies, see different outcomes, and look at different ways of working as a team."[7] For firefighters, police, and medical crews, the value of such highly specific training for dangerous situations is hard to measure.

This is just one example of using the "otherworldliness" of the Metaverse to bridge digital and physical reality. If the life-endangering circumstances that engage first responders can be emulated with more interactivity and less physical risk—imagine the options on a larger scale. Not only that, the Metaverse's versatility puts in perspective how effective the platform can be used in more everyday instances such as customer service, sales, and retail roles.

PixelMax's co-founder, Shay O'Carroll, describes how they use a game model for medical training in the Metaverse. "The game becomes the learning activity. In the medical world, we've used gamified technologies to train lab technicians; you'll break out in different groups and then go to, say, a virtual PCR testing machine, where you'll go through stages of learning about how to operate that machine, with your training result recorded."[8]

Like the NBA coaches, O'Carroll understands the lifelike quality of virtual training is something to be leveraged with Metaverse users for educational opportunities that appeal to every age, style, and capacity of learner. Since the genesis of the Internet 2.0, our attention spans continue to diminish. Social media platforms now favor brief snippets of video content that give us the dopamine high we crave. This constant chemical reaction is evolutionarily changing our brains, reflecting in the way we process information and, inevitably, the way we do business. While this sociological shift might present attention deficit issues in a traditional setting, the Metaverse is coming at a time where it can accommodate these sociological changes. By making learning materials goal-based (think trivia, scavenger hunts, competitive group games), the brain will stay engaged on learning the material in audio, visual, and tangible form—while also getting a dopamine hit.

Ever since Apple rolled out Siri on the iPhone in the early 2010s, the way we find out new things has changed forever. The evolved verbal commands became so engrained in us that

Amazon and Google followed suit with interactive home controls that can do everything from setting a home security alarm to making a grocery list. From there it's not a huge leap to the learning environment of the Metaverse, geared toward personalizing our goals to help us reach our highest professional potential. Beyond preparing us for our first day on the job or leveling us up for our big promotion, the Metaverse provides a sense of fun that the traditional Western workplace has never seen. This playfulness may meet resistance with American workers, because it has been engrained in us to strive, but the more we can get out of our old mentality and get into the game, then the more we can evolve as learners and employees—and enjoy ourselves in the process.

The Versatile Classroom

Imagine it's Friday afternoon and you have class in the Metaverse. Your avatar walks onto the digital campus of your organization. To your left you see a calendar of the events scheduled for that day. Flicking through the calendar notes, you can find out who will be lecturing on what topic, and any additional material for the course that you might need. As your pixelated self shuffles behind other avatars heading into the auditorium, you can already tell the session is going to be well attended. Several blocks of seating are already taken; the seminar has capacity for four hundred or four thousand people from all over the world, as the walls can be pushed back to accommodate more participants.

The screen beyond the stage is set up in presentation mode, and near the podium you see a cluster of avatars standing in a circle, chatting via voice conversation in real time as they prepare to start the session. As an attendee, you control the ability to raise your hand to ask a question; to chat in a private or public message box to speak with other class members attending the seminar; and to use your microphone, in case you are called upon to contribute. If the training program is well designed, you will be.

This is something I've come to see in working with Metaverse training programs throughout the years: the capacity for engagement is huge and highly significant. Because the digital platform offers such lifelikeness during meetings, it requires a high level of thoughtfulness, attentiveness, and participation. Remaining a passive spectator in the Metaverse is like sitting in the airport and never getting on a plane.

Not only does the Metaverse enable us to engage one-on-one, but it also enables us to teach with dimension and to archive every topic we talk about. This means the log of Metaverse trainings can be revisited at a later time; all employees have to do is go into a digital library to find them. This translates to the opportunity of generating complex educational content regularly. An organization might have its "core onboarding" content, but a digital platform provides the space for educational evergreens: an ongoing collection on the industry (and how to thrive in it) as the organization evolves. This beautifully "canonizes" some of the cornerstone materials of the company, including digital meetings held with a founder at the start that determine things like core values, company direction, and brand management.

Having these materials chronicled and available serves only to be able to build on them as the years pass.

The learning environment can be tailored to match the organization or material, too. For a corporate gathering, virtual auditoriums are ideal; for the NBA, stadiums are a clear match. Firehouses, operating rooms, construction sites—all of these environments can be built in the Metaverse to offer abundance in terms of experiential learning.

Take warehouses as an example. According to information about use cases from online resource Warehouse DT through a video, "Amazon Robotics Builds Digital Twins of Warehouses," the Amazon workforce across more than two hundred fulfillment centers handles tens of millions of packages each and every day. It is a complex operation, with over half a million mobile drive robots supporting warehouse logistics. Now, Amazon Robotics is building digital twins of their warehouses through NVIDIA's Omniverse platform.[9] Productivity remains at an all-time high because there is no downtime for the warehouse. Before, the company would have had to interrupt operations to give in-person demonstrations during orientation. Now, an immersive virtual experience proves more efficient. Alongside the productivity benefits, the Metaverse model offers a huge leap forward for safety education and training. The digital twin method allows for interactive training in a variety of areas, such as lifting heavy materials and using machinery. Real-time feedback on posture helps individuals practice safe movement.

Many conventional service-sector companies do not offer extensive training programs. Motivated professionals take it upon themselves to invest in their professional development through taking classes and attending webinars, reading industry magazines and blogs, listening to relevant podcasts, and seeking out advisors and mentors. For instance, it is relatively rare to have access to a structured, curated, always-available source of professional training, as I have seen offered so effectively through the Metaverse.

Image courtesy of Virbela

International digital platforms give employees the opportunity to interact with seasoned professionals throughout the industry in any location. They experience the strong advantage of exchanging regional procedures and protocols among like-minded colleagues. Through an array of seminars on everything from cold-pitching and compliance, to attracting online clients, to navigating advances in the virtual sphere—the doors of the Metaverse are always open to those seeking growth and knowledge.

In those days when traveling played a larger role in our access to education, professionals would traverse the world to learn about developing practices. Seeking to enhance their skill set or perhaps become a "next-generation professional," participants would often document every session they attended on the latest trends, technologies, or traps for the unwary, scribbling detailed notes furiously about a subject until the notebook had no more empty space, the pen no more ink, or the hand no more strength. And then the conference would end and their enthusiasm would wind down—even before the trip home, when the magic of the experience, as well as the knowledge gained, would inevitably fade away without implementation.

As organizations lean into the Metaverse, they can provide a steady diet of these experiences. No more peaking and crashing over hyped-up professional development opportunities. When you care about the longevity of your people's educational experiences, you want them to be sustained with knowledge, not fed information in tiny, charged bites. Supporting them in this way will keep you ahead of your industry's evolutionary curve.

I am always struck by how often employees step up to contribute to professional development in the Metaverse. "Hey, is someone teaching a class on client engagement? If not, I would like to do that." The key is to fully trust and empower them to be participants in shaping the professional development landscape of the organization. Such was the experience of Rose Burke in Oklahoma City. Rose leveraged the Metaverse platform to bolster her already strong credentials as an agent educator and mentor running weekly Masterminds in the eXp Metaverse campus; through these kinds of events, many agents have honed their skills, expanded their perspective, and built lasting camaraderie.

Change is the one great constant in business. Though the pace may shift depending on an organization's orientation and region, recognizing this is core to the preparedness of a business for future success. This is another reason why early adoption of the Metaverse is so important, even if it causes initial discomfort; good business leaders know longevity requires their organization to remain relevant. Though virtual reality has seemed "out there" since its genesis, the era of its worldwide implementation is near; the future of business can be learned with the click of a button. Business leaders should acknowledge this and utilize virtual training to their best advantage.

The Rising Workforce

We don't talk much about the alpha generation (Gen A) in the workplace—perhaps because as of 2023, they are only ten years old. But in the next seven years, these children will graduate from high school and either go to college or join the workforce. It's imperative we appeal to them as prospective and tech-savvy employees because most of them know more about progressive technology than those of us who were around at the birth of the internet. Is our training and professional development strategy ready for them?

Given the expertise of these "digital native" workers, we must embrace reverse intergenerational learning and celebrate the fact that new recruits have much to teach us. We are entering an era where experience with computers will be more valuable to the job market than degrees and certifications. This leverage alone will make late millennials, zoomers, and alphas the top competitors for jobs in the virtual workforce.

In turn, Metaverse-based companies will be challenged to appeal to a demographic who has grown up in a 3-D, digitally connected environment. Members of Gen Z and Gen A will be the greatest asset among hires, so long as employers can incentivize them with competitive pay, promising perks, and professional development plans.

Their radical embrace of these technologies will lead to the longevity of an organization, as more seasoned workers will have the opportunity to learn from the more technologically advanced. Where the first group brings the traditions such as the importance of loyalty to a company and of contributing to its collective character, the second will further our command of the digital terrain, taking virtual work and learning to make transcendent, generative, and innovative spaces.

IN BRIEF

The opportunities for learning in the Metaverse are huge. Training in the Metaverse offers saturated engagement through dynamic role-play via gamified learning technology; it is "learning via doing" in every regard, and it is available to employees no matter where they are located.

Image courtesy of Virbela

12

EMBRACING ENVIRONMENTAL SUSTAINABILITY

The World's Biggest Remote-Work Experiment

I'm looking at an aerial photo of Boston's Back Bay neighborhood. In it the sky is bright despite a fine layer of cloud cover, the John Hancock Tower and Prudential Tower are both shining columns rising above crisp lines of red brick row houses, and the Charles River shimmers its way through the heart of the city.

The photo is, in a real sense, a snapshot in time. It was taken in early 2020 as the coronavirus pandemic first took a hold on the nation, and soon after then-Governor Charlie Baker issued a stay-at-home advisory. Seemingly overnight, the morning rush hour virtually disappeared—and Boston University researchers found that the city air became clearer just as fast.

According to the article "No, It's Not Your Imagination, the Air in Boston Is Cleaner," one Boston University professor who monitors air pollutants around Boston and Massachusetts found that carbon emissions in Boston overall fell by an estimated 15 percent in the month following the advisory on March 23—an effect, according to the researcher, in line with implementing the city's most aggressive emissions reduction policies.[1]

Like that idyllic photo of a gleaming Boston neighborhood, the effect is also a snapshot in time, capturing a dramatic change in human behavior in response to a singular crisis. However, the research warned that these measures wouldn't have a lasting effect due to a lack of long-term plans for decreasing carbon emissions, but if we can learn from our experience from the pandemic to leverage work-from-home models and decrease daily commutes, that could change.[2]

Far beyond the borders of Massachusetts, when organizations vacated their brick-and-mortar office spaces, environmental scientists observed a plunge in energy and emission reductions on a global level. The world saw a brief yet significant reduction in global CO_2 emissions in April 2020, with mobility, production, and consumption patterns experiencing dramatic shifts that led to a 17 percent decrease compared to peak 2019 levels. **A team from the London School of Economics described the pandemic as "the largest remote work experiment in human history."**[3]

This inspired a Spanish team of researchers to study the reduction of nitrogen dioxide, the main pollutant generated by traffic emissions, in the atmosphere of larger international cities as workplaces opened up again. They concluded that even moderate levels of working from home would still generate a reduction in air pollution of around 8 percent. As innovation consultant Adi Gaskell observes, "While consuming digital resources, such as video conferencing, burns a considerable amount of energy in data centers, the researchers argue that the net impact is still positive, with Zoom calls emitting just 0.6 percent of the carbon emissions generated on a typical commute."[4]

The Spanish group determined that congested cities could significantly improve global air quality through the embrace of digital workspaces. The group's takeaway was that "if we are able to enhance teleworking and reduce traffic emissions so drastically and promptly to stop the spread of the COVID-19, we are capable of taking similar measures to stop other deadly diseases related to the poor air-quality in cities."[5]

To be crystal clear—this research team, like others around the world, described the risk of poor air quality using the same term they used to describe the pandemic: *deadly.*

The ozone layer impacts the air we breathe, water we drink, plants we grow, and animals we farm. According to the United States Environmental Protection Agency, air toxics (also known as toxic air pollutants or hazardous air pollutants) can cause chronic and fatal diseases including cancer, respiratory problems, reduced fertility, developmental disorders, and neurological malfunctioning. Air quality directly impacts every worker within every organization—whether they realize it or not. (And whether they choose to politicize it or not.)

You may be a climate change skeptic, but the impact of air pollutants on human health has been examined in detail over a long period of time. The problems of polluted air were documented over two thousand years ago. In Imperial Rome, civil engineer Frontinus (ca. AD 96) believed that his contribution to aqueducts and fountains helped make the air cleaner: "The causes of the unwholesome atmosphere, which gave the air of the City so bad a name with the ancients, are now removed."[6]

Is there any better "health benefits" package than reducing the risk of disease and suffering?

The Race Starts Now

Despite the robust body of research that continues to accumulate on the subject of climate change, some businesspeople still consider the topic politically inflammatory and reject the scientific evidence as a whole. Yet the reasons to make environmental sustainability a pillar of your organization's values are threefold:

1. The credibility of your organization with customers, investors, and employees (current and prospective) depends on it.

2. Compliance with frameworks such as Environmental Social Governance (ESG) is necessary.

3. Sustainability is now recognized as a value that is entirely compatible with, and often contributes to, profitability.

Entire books have been written on the topic of why businesses should pay attention to environmental matters. In this chapter, my interest is in describing the natural match between a Metaverse work model and sustainability, so I will simply provide a thumbnail overview of ESG to set the scene for how the (virtual) Metaverse can benefit our (physical) planet—if thoughtfully applied.

One definition of ESG that I find useful comes from RE Tech Advisors, an ESG advisory firm: "ESG is the now well-known acronym for a framework that focuses stakeholders on environmental, social, and governance risks and opportunities."[7] The purpose of ESG reporting is to offer transparency into an organization's ESG activities and to measure its sustainability performance so stakeholders—such as investors, consumers, and future employees—can make informed decisions.

Each letter of the acronym represents a bracket of organizational responsibilities.

E for "environmental" encapsulates assessment of climate risk, natural resource conservation, pollution and waste, possible environmental opportunities, and the element of environmental justice.

S for "social" includes human capital, diversity, equity and inclusion, product liability, community investment and social opportunity, and employee privacy.

G for "governance" is comprised of cybersecurity and data controls, corporate governance, behavior, purpose, third-party vendor codes, ethics, and executive compensation.

Certainly, there are more categories and subcategories beneath each letter, and they will continue to expand as ESG is adopted more widely.

In the US, there are currently no mandatory ESG disclosure

requirements on the federal level. However, the increasing number of mandatory ESG regulations around the world means that more and more US companies are being asked by stakeholders to disclose their data. The number of nations that introduced legislation making ESG reporting mandatory in the past year proves that ESG reporting is not just a trend; it is here to stay.

One South Korean start-up is modeling a more sustainable kind of office space in the Metaverse. Zigbang is partially funded by the South Korean government as part of their initiative to support beginning enterprises to meet ESG goals set by the United Nations. Zigbang launched its virtual office space offering "Soma world" in mid-2022. There, companies can lease space in PropTech Tower. A few months after opening, two thousand people from twenty global and domestic companies were working inside the thirty-story building. "A company based in the Metaverse dramatically reduces the carbon footprint of a workplace that may include everything from transportation used during the commute to work, to office supplies like pen and paper in everyday office life," explained government spokesperson Minjo Chun.[8]

Being ahead of the game on ESG disclosure regulation makes sound business sense. Deloitte offers the view that "boards and C-suites that can get ahead of ESG disclosure regulation can build a business that meaningfully integrates ESG into its strategic planning and is better poised to manage risks, while also delivering shareholder value and increasing their organizations' resiliency in a changed world."[9]

Consider recruitment as just one facet of that future resiliency.

Because millennials and Gen Z are Left-leaning, "value driven" talent, they will prioritize working for mission-driven workspaces (even if it means taking longer to secure a job). These generations will be able to discern whether an organization is truly prioritizing global change or is simply out to "tick all the boxes." Leaders who are passive in their adoption of ESG are likely going to miss out on exceptional hires.

There are so many reasons to apply ESG concepts now and ensure sustainability protocols are scalable. And to understand that (as the team at PwC puts it), "ESG is more than good intentions. It's about creating a tangible, practical plan that achieves real results. Success is not about climate change, diversity, and disclosures alone. It's about embedding these principles—and more across your business—from investment to sustainable innovation."[10]

Going All In

I would argue that our future depends on exploring the many ways a virtual location (the Metaverse) may positively impact a physical location (our planet). To start with, here are three avenues where I see this occurring, most often with relatively little effort (or cost) required:

1. Apply a remote work model.

2. Reduce long-distance travel.

3. Achieve a minimal "office footprint."

Working from home intuitively feels like it must be better for the environment. All those traffic emissions—gone. Right? But if an organization is looking to increase their sustainability through a remote work model, their best option is to "go all in." While some scholars argue that any change is better than no change (just look at the part-time commute statistics), others believe that the hybrid work model isn't the answer. By blending home- and office-based working, we must duplicate the equipment required for each employee to do their job. During the pandemic, we saw a spike in purchases of laptops (by over 11 percent) and home office furniture (more than 300 percent).[11] Even the demand for more rooms and overall space in the home rose, with a flurry of extensions and mini-renovations as families sought more square footage to combine work and life more comfortably. And as we know, excess consumption has an environmental cost due to increased factory emissions, depletion of natural resources, and an escalation in waste.

The environmental downside of a hybrid work model is also due in part to the fact that no company can enforce sustainability in the lifestyles of their employees—and I would argue, nor should they. If companies could ensure every employee recycles, drives less, uses electric cars, and relies on solar panels, it would be a different conversation. But there's a reasonable risk that employees who work from home part time might actually be generating *more* toxic waste.

Remember, too, that buildings that sit empty still use energy. Many businesses with a hybrid work model keep their office headquarters open five days per week and leave it up to the employee to choose their in-office days. The reality is that most on-site offices are voraciously energy hungry, even when the desks are unoccupied. Take it from FULL Creative, an organization that makes programs, platforms, and tools for virtual work clients. Their motto reflects their commitment to virtual work: "Work is what you do, not where you do it." In 2008, FULL began considering ways to become more eco-friendly through the redistribution of resources. They made the realization that "buildings still use some energy whether anyone's in them or not. So leaving our homes empty during the day, and offices empty at night, is just plain wasteful. We can do better."[12] With a goal to be more energy efficient, FULL revamped their work model.

Long before many businesses were thinking much about digital platforms, FULL tripled their work force yet slashed their office space by more than half. They went from a hundred employees in an office of more than 10,000 square feet to three hundred US employees with office space of less than 4,000 square feet. They did it by taking their own medicine—doubling down on every virtual work tool and strategy that applied to their business. Now their team is distributed across the US, the UK, Canada, and India.

FULL quickly learned that striving to make a positive environmental impact can help companies add value long term. More employees. More expansion. More profit. That said, a great deal of forethought went into progressing FULL's workspace, which is something businesses looking to transition should consider.

Early on in my Metaverse work life, we aimed to cultivate the kind of eco-aware atmosphere that could be methodically replicated by any business leader seeking to transition to a virtual platform. In the case of eXp, the company made "radical" sacrifices from the beginning, committing corporately to being 100 percent virtual. As an industry disruptor, eXp did not own any corporate real estate, nor did we require agents to own, rent or otherwise pay for physical office space. We ran all operations through the Cloud, leveraging the Metaverse platform to empower agents, partners, and clients alike. While our corporate footprint was entirely virtual, we had countless agents across markets who would *choose* to secure office space on their own—branding it in the way that they wanted (subject to regulation) and making their own determination as to square footage, location, utility, cost, length of term, and so on. Personally, I wasn't anti-office. What I took issue with most and take issue with today in numerous service industries is telling an employee that they need to subsidize spending decisions that are completely out of their own control and which oftentimes defy logic, such as exercising office expansion rights even when nobody is coming into the primary space to begin with.

When airlines shut down in 2021 to stop the spread of COVID-19, eXp's leadership team was prompted to explore even more eco-friendly ways of connecting. While some were reluctant to eliminate in-person interaction entirely, it presented an opportunity to—virtually—become more creative and innovative than ever before.

As I described in the previous chapter, eXp began utilizing its main auditorium in more engaging ways, leaning even further into the Metaverse and the boundless functions of its campus. Once team members embraced the experience of virtual seminars and meetings in the comfort of their own homes, they appreciated that business trips are actually quite taxing and hardly worth stealing time away from their families and lives outside of work.

Business flights are a major contributor to carbon emissions, in part because of the sheer number of flights taken by employees versus vacationers. For example, in 2019 the global software company Salesforce racked up 146,000 metric tons of CO_2 emissions through business travel alone.[13] That's roughly the amount produced by 17,500 US homes over the same time span. Keep in mind the likelihood that many business travelers are sitting in first class, where the CO_2 footprint is about four times as much as economy.[14]

In scenarios like this, the pursuit of sustainability is a lost cause—along with the pursuit of fiscal responsibility.

The list of other spin-off benefits to the environment from a Metaverse workplace is long. We all know how it goes: if we're out and about, we typically purchase more things, create more trash, and use more fuel and energy. It's the after-work coffee, the vending machine snack, the time our cars sit idling in traffic, and having to own more clothing and objects for two work identities. Workers not having to purchase clothing and goods to "look presentable" or "keep their office space" is a sustainable initiative all on its own. As is a work model where employees can make their own lunches every day, rather than relying upon drive-thrus at fast food joints that only offer nonbiodegradable packaging. There are so many small benefits that make up the greater whole—if organizations choose to go all in.

That's why I say: if you're going to take the leap, do rigorous research, plan accordingly—then *take it*.

But What about the Energy Cost of Data?

The contribution of the Metaverse to sustainability cannot go entirely unquestioned, even by an enthusiast such as myself. While it's true that a virtual work model can reduce carbon emissions generated by car, train, and air travel, it's also true that the Metaverse will require high computing power and broadband speed, which you would expect to increase power consumption. However, two prominent scholars in the field of technology, energy use, and the environment have challenged the perception that giant tech companies with power-hungry data centers are necessarily environmental villains. In a 2021 study, Jonathan Koomey and Eric Masanet set out to inject a "dose of reality" into widely held assumptions. They point out that many researchers "are not familiar with fast-changing computer technology—processing, memory, storage, and networks. In making predictions, they tend to underestimate the pace of energy-saving innovation and how the systems work."[15] In their analysis, the authors cite two large international network operators, Spain's Telefónica and US-based Cogent, and their reported data traffic and energy use for the pandemic year of 2020. Telefónica handled a 45 percent jump in data through its network with no increase in energy use. Cogent's electricity use fell 21 percent even as data traffic increased 38 percent.

"Yes, we're using a lot more data services and putting a lot more data through networks," Koomey says of the study. "But we're also getting a lot more efficient very quickly." Even so, they cautioned against trying to predict too far into the future based on their findings. The complexity, dynamism, and unpredictability of technology development and markets, Koomey and Masanat say, make it unwise to project out more than two or three years. As they put it, you can't simply "extrapolate to Doomsday."[16]

Championing a sustainable work culture means directing the attention of the whole organization to clear eco-conscious objectives. However, in the evolving and often emotionally charged space of environmentalism, goals can seem nebulous or muddled. In an effort to strip away confusion, a group of behavioral scientists from the London School of Economics and Political Science (LSE) offers four specific operational areas for organizations to consider. "We highlight four behavioral domains that are particularly important: energy, travel, technology, and waste. Behavioral change across these domains can have major environmental impacts when aggregated across individuals, teams, companies, and industries."

Ganga Shreedhar, Kate Laffan, and Laura M. Giurge of LSE go on to draw out a method for championing a sustainable Metaverse work culture. They note the importance of leadership engaging their workers about individual values, passions, interests, and drives before determining the collective "goal."[17]

No two organizations are the same, therefore no two sustainability journeys are the same. The LSE professors advise tailoring the established policies of an organization to the functions of their eco-minded work culture, emphasizing "a one-size-fits-all approach won't work" for all Metaverse workspaces. "For example, one company's workforce might rely heavily on technology, so helping reduce emissions from e-waste and energy is especially important. Another company's workforce might commute long distances or undertake frequent work travel; for this company the priorities should be to lower travel emissions by reducing options like non-essential trips, using low-carbon transport, flying economy for essential trips, and carbon offsetting."[18]

The best conversations about promoting sustainability in a Metaverse workplace can be had by engaging every member of the organization and by getting creative, leaving no stone unturned. Shreedhar, Laffan, and Giurge point to behaviors such as supporting employees to change to renewable sources of energy at home by providing access to auto-switching energy services, or providing recycling and safe disposal of duplicate or old electronic devices and e-waste through in-house drop-off centers.

Ray Anderson—best known as a carpet manufacturer but also a dedicated sustainability advocate—said back in 2009, **"We have a choice to make during our brief visit to this beautiful blue and green living planet: to hurt it or to help it."**[19] As an organization develops its Metaverse workplace strategy, they have a choice to build it on a social justice foundation, embracing accessibility, inclusiveness, and equality as well as environmental sustainability. But to do that, business leaders must do more than pay lip service to environmental principles; they must actively engage to ensure their version of the Metaverse develops in a sustainable way. Leaders willing to strive toward sustainability need to understand the intricate and unique impact of *their* industry, sector, and organization on the atmosphere. Only then can we collectively make energized, impactful, and effective global change.

IN BRIEF

Is there any better "health benefits" package than reducing the risk of disease and suffering? As an organization develops its Metaverse workplace strategy, they can choose to embrace environmental sustainability through reduced travel, commuting, and office footprint. But to make an impact, business leaders must do more than pay lip service to environmental principles.

Image courtesy of Virbela

CONCLUSION

IN THIS BOOK, I've set out to offer you a framework for building a unified organizational culture that can dominate in its industry, while at the same time valuing its people. As you go about implementing that framework, I urge you to start the way you plan to continue. We have one chance to build this new work environment on a foundation of social justice. Right from the beginning, let's bake in the things that matter, rather than find ourselves several years down the road trying to retrofit our values.

Along the way, I've referred to "values" many times. It occurs to me now that the word "value" has another aspect that is relevant to our thinking about the Metaverse workplace. No matter what business you are in, you have certain assets at your disposal. Money. Land. Knowledge. Relationships. People. Unless you value them, treating them with respect and acknowledging their worth, you will almost certainly fritter them away without ever seeing them fulfill their potential.

I'm convinced that the Metaverse workplace is the way of the future. The fact is, it's already here, and you ignore it at your own risk. Right now, we finally get to live the future we've been imagining since we were young, but the best part is this: it's not by way of videogames; it is through a new digital revolution that will expand our work potential past anything we've ever dreamed. The Metaverse is not something that's going to negatively impact us, rot our brains, or keep us from work. It provides the opportunity to evolve into a better form of work that yields a higher profit margin so we can focus on purpose-driven business missions.

In this new era of work, the standard business practices of past decades no longer apply. As a fellow business leader, I challenge you to be more than a spectator and to join the front line of leaders who are ensuring the Metaverse develops in a sustainable way. I challenge you to work together with your peers, with government, and with your employees to shape a Metaverse that drives results while at the same time valuing its people.

AFTERWORD

I WRITE THIS afterword while sitting on a plane early in a flight from Phoenix, Arizona, to my home in Boston on August 10, 2023—some 18 months after I first began to work on this book. My visit to Arizona, much like prior visits to Utah in the preceding months, only further reinforces for me the transformative nature of the Metaverse as a workplace and the strength of the appetite for such transformation across the professional services industries, in particular, the legal profession.

My Arizona trip included a series of very enjoyable meetings in which I was able to share my experience and perspective on the destructive impact of fixed brick-and-mortar and redundant staffing costs on access to justice and affordable representation, on the quality of that representation, and on the physical and emotional well-being of the legal profession's members including, undoubtedly, some of its most talented, reputable, and "successful" practitioners.

In late 2009, I was seven years into my career as a practicing attorney at a midsize Boston law firm. We had a newborn and a two-year-old at the time, and at those ages they were often asleep when I began my grueling drive into the city in the morning and again when I would return in the evening. I was weary, unhappy, and battle scarred from the daily routine in an industry that rarely, if ever, experiences innovation and that operates in a business model that discourages efficiency through hourly billing. Why take only 1 hour to do what you could in 12 when you are required to hit 1,800 billable hours in a year?

Who pays for this inefficiency? The clients certainly do—oftentimes resulting in additional attorneys added to a call or peripheral, even irrelevant, issues to the client or their objectives being raised. When the ebb and flow of economic conditions and/or demand for types of legal services trigger law firms (even if subconsciously) to drive greater revenue through even greater inefficiency, there is a fundamental and foundational problem for anyone who believes in the virtues of legal representation and expanding access to justice. Someone has to pay for the mahogany conference room table at which people rarely now sit given technological advances and trends towards hybrid or remote work. Someone has to pay for the ornate furnishings, gourmet lunches, and the revolving art exhibits that adorn the walls. It's pretty easy to identify clients as the responsible party for such arbitrary spending decisions on inessentials that, in an earlier time, may have caused attorneys to feel better about themselves and their place in life and may have even impressed prospective clients into signing an engagement letter. It doesn't take any expertise to see that the client foots the bill. That was certainly my belief as an attorney in late 2009.

However, fourteen years later I know that it wasn't just the clients that paid for the inefficiency and extravagance of law firms. It was the attorney. It was the service professional. It was me. Legal professionals bore the burden in ways that were financial, sacrificial, detrimental to true presence among family and friends, and lethal to any hope for a balanced life, but the noble belief in the law for the good it enabled—the energetic and hopeful idealism that causes so many to enter law school in the first place—didn't fade and disappear entirely from view.

My eXp experience leads me to the inescapable conclusion that by eliminating traditional infrastructure and working together in the Metaverse, law firms not only could succeed in difficult times but, if executed well, could offer a compensation model that could be disruptive to one of the largest industries in the United States economy and one that substantively serves as the foundation for everything else. Resources that traditionally would be allocated to maintaining traditional and hierarchical organizational structure can now be reallocated and reinvested in the very people who are actually doing the work and generating the revenues—the lawyers themselves.

Today, a strong majority of attorneys graduate law school with more than $100,000 in student loan debt. They take home on average between 20–25 percent of what they bill out with 75 percent of revenues allocated to sumptuous spaces of diminishing utility (to the client and the professional), redundant staffing, and arbitrary spending decisions for items with no intrinsic value to the services they provide or the clientele for whom they provide those services. Legal professionals today rank among the most stressed, overworked, depressed, sleep-deprived, and misery filled professionals of any industry. Junior lawyers aspire to the prestige of Partner status, until they're leveraged or exploited by Partners and management on a poorly illuminated path, which is often lacking in any objective criteria or transparency and for which the timeframe of advancement often seems a moving target.

In the event Partner status is achieved, often the first thing the Partner is asked to do is write a check for a capital contribution, oftentimes well into the six figures. Then, they continue to bill. Perhaps profits will be distributed. Perhaps they won't. They will bill in excess for many more years—without anything to show for it beyond the initial morale boost and sense of achievement. They will bill and bill oftentimes until their passing. They will come into their white-shoe firm before dawn and depart after midnight, leaving barely enough time for two hours of sleep, a chance to say a silent goodbye to sleeping family members, and a short shower before having to return to the office . . . and to billing. Their clients don't want to speak with them because the moment the conversation begins they are being billed in six-minute increments at ever increasing hourly rates. When client and counselor do interact, it is generally because the client has a problem—a problem big enough to justify the expense of the call. Oftentimes, and justifiably, those problems make the client unhappy. Unhappiness is contagious and self-injurious. Many a day is spent consumed by an uninterrupted series of conversations with unhappy people. It becomes easy to lose any sight of a possible future. It's easy to begin drinking excessively to numb the misery. It's easy to deteriorate physically and mentally.

Since mid-January 2023, I have been assembling a team of some of the most talented people I have come across in pursuit of offering a remedy to these systemic and structural challenges. Together, we have developed an approach to and philosophy around private law practice that can cut billable hour requirements in half; facilitate alternative pricing models for clients that are more efficient, more predictable, and encourage engagement; more than double attorney compensation, not including that derived from an objective, apolitical, and abbreviated path to partnership income; restore relationships, balance, and health; and create an opportunity to rediscover the long-obscured but enduring desire to serve their clients, their communities, and the greater good in the most fulfilling ways.

It was from these efforts that OMNUS was born and which, with any luck, will launch just before this book is released. We've had incredible opportunities to share both the problem and the solution with present and former members of congress, state attorneys general, state supreme court justices, Silicon Valley legends, and state house speakers. The attorneys who we speak with in markets across the country immediately identify with the pain of inefficiency, its consequences, and the desperate need for a solution, and, particularly on the elected official side, they are beyond enthusiastic about what we propose and what it can represent for all stakeholders.

Back in 2009 once I understood that the service professional was paying for inefficiency and excess, I knew eXp would achieve great things. The Metaverse advantages of efficiency and community building are just that pronounced. I staked everything on eXp's success and in the belief in my own ability to meaningfully and favorably impact that outcome. I wouldn't trade the experience or the friendships. I am also excited about the future, believing the benefits and opportunities of Metaverse-based services are just beginning to come into view. To my own astonishment, with OMNUS, I find myself, in just eight short months, on the precipice of something that I believe, with even greater conviction than I did in 2009, will be transformative and enormously successful by its own definitions. With eXp, the journey was more valuable and rewarding than the destination. I am ready for the next journey to begin. The hero of that journey and the story that might form from it years from now will unwaveringly be the service professional. OMNUS will be the guide. Thank you for reading.

—Jason Gesing
August 10, 2023

NOTES

Chapter 1: Where Pivoting Meets Profit

1. Jennifer Moss, "The Pandemic Changed Us. Now Companies Have to Change Too," *Harvard Business Review*, July 1, 2022, https://hbr.org/2022/07/the-pandemic-changed-us-now-companies-have-to-change-too.

2. Molly Sloan, "Netflix vs Blockbuster—3 Key Takeaways," *Drift*, June 1, 2020, https://www.drift.com/blog/netflix-vs-blockbuster/.

3. Alexander Fernandez, "The Metaverse: The Future of Work," *Forbes*, March 18, 2022, https://www.forbes.com/sites/forbesbusinesscouncil/2022/03/18/the-metaverse-the-future-of-work/?sh=3de78334267e+%3A.

4. Fernandez, "The Metaverse."

Chapter 2: The Great Equalizer 2.0

1. Fastco Works, "Why the Metaverse?" *Fast Company*, accessed August 2, 2023, https://www.fastcompany.com/90790147/why-the-metaverse.

2. Fastco Works, "Why the Metaverse?"

3. Nir Kshetri, "5 Challenges of Taking College Classes in the Metaverse," *Fast Company*, September 19, 2022, accessed November 16, 2022, https://www.fastcompany.com/90790011/5-challenges-of-taking-college-classes-in-the-metaverse.

Chapter 3: Transparency and Lifting the Curtain

1. Mike Kappel, "Transparency in Business: 5 Ways to Build Trust," *Forbes*, April 3, 2019, https://www.forbes.com/sites/mikekappel/2019/04/03/transparency-in-business-5-ways-to-build-trust/?sh=2bc206766149.

2. "How to Create a Culture of Transparency in a Virtual Work Environment (and Why You Should)," TriNet, February 14, 2018, https://www.trinet.com/insights/how-to-create-a-culture-of-transparency-in-a-virtual-work-environment-and-why-you-should.

3. Kevin Eikenberry and Wayne Turmel, *The Long-Distance Leader* (Oakland, CA: Berrett-Koehler, 2018), 141.

Chapter 4: Building a Secure Workplace

1. Tiffany Xingyu Wang, "Here's How We Can Build a Sustainable Metaverse," *Al Majalla*, last updated April 15, 2022, https://en.majalla.com/node/216141/technologyhere%E2%80%99s-how-we-can-build-sustainable-metaverse.

2. ExpressVPN, "Survey Reveals Surveillance Fears over the Metaverse Workplace," June 13, 2022, https://www.expressvpn.com/blog/survey-reveals-surveillance-fears-over-the-metaverse-workplace/#key.

3. ExpressVPN, "Survey Reveals Surveillance Fears"

4. ExpressVPN, "Survey Reveals Surveillance Fears"

5. Mark van Rijmenam, "Solutions to Drive Safety and Privacy in the Metaverse with Tiffany Xingyu Wang," *Step into the Metaverse* episode 33 (podcast), January 17, 2023, https://www.thedigitalspeaker.com/solutions-safety-privacy-metaverse-tiffany-xingyu-wang-step-into-the-metaverse-podcast-ep33/.

6. PricewaterhouseCoopers, "Trust and Risks in the Metaverse: 6 Key Considerations," accessed December 29, 2022, https://www.pwc.com/us/en/tech-effect/emerging-tech/metaverse-trust-and-risk-considerations.html.

7. PricewaterhouseCoopers, "Trust and Risks in the Metaverse."

8. Eric Jang, "Ready Employee One: Data Privacy within the Metaverse," OnLabor, June 24, 2022, https://onlabor.org/ready-employee-one-data-privacy-within-the-metaverse/.

9. "Virbela," eXp World Holdings, accessed July 8, 2023, https://expworldholdings.com/our-businesses/virbela/.

10. "The Future of Work: Tech Leaders Talk about the Shift to Virtual Offices," *Virbela* (blog), accessed July 8, 2023, https://www.virbela.com/blog/the-future-of-work-tech-leaders-talk-about-the-shift-to-virtual-offices.

Chapter 5: Top-Down Accountability

1. Wisconsin School of Business, "Driven to Distraction—What Causes Cyberloafing at Work?" press release, June 25, 2015, https://business.wisc.edu/news/driven-to-distraction-what-causes-cyberloafing-at-work/.

2. Jason Fried and David Heinemeier Hansson, *Remote: Office Not Required* (New York: Crown, 2013).

3. Yogesh K. Dwivedi et al., "Metaverse beyond the Hype: Multidisciplinary Perspectives on Emerging Challenges, Opportunities, and Agenda for Research, Practice and Policy," *International Journal of Information Management* 66 (October 2022): 102542, https://doi.org/10.1016/j.ijinfomgt.2022.102542.

4. Richard Branson, "Flexible Working Is Smart Working," Richard Branson's blog, February 2, 2015, https://www.virgin.com/branson-family/richard-branson-blog/flexible-working-smart-working.

5. Aimee Groth, "Richard Branson Says That Marissa Mayer Got It Wrong about Remote Employees," *Business Insider*, February 25, 2013, https://www.businessinsider.com/richard-branson-says-that-marissa-mayer-got-it-wrong-about-remote-employees-2013-2.

6. Fried and Hansson, *Remote*.

7. Richard Branson, "Give People the Freedom of Where to Work," *Richard Branson's Blog*, quoted in Andres Jauregui, "Richard Branson Criticizes Yahoo, Marissa

Mayer Over Work-From-Home Ban," *HuffPost*,
February 25, 2013, https://www.huffpost.com/entry/
richard-branson-yahoo-marissa-mayer_n_2759243.

Chapter 6: Achieving Peak Productivity

1. Jack Kelly, "CEOs Will Be Clamping Down on Employees,"
   Forbes, January 30, 2023, https://www.forbes.com/sites/
   jackkelly/2023/01/30/ceos-will-be-clamping-down-on-
   employees/?sh=6a8a347d10db.

2. Larry English, "Why a Great Remote Leadership Strategy
   Is a Cure for Quiet Quitting," *Forbes*, September 20, 2022,
   https://www.forbes.com/sites/larryenglish/2022/09/20/
   why-a-great-remote-leadership-strategy-is-a-cure-for-quiet-
   quitting/?sh=16e1d0526a46.

3. English, "Why a Great Remote Leadership Strategy."

Chapter 7: A (Virtual) Level Playing Field

1. Curt Rice, "How Blind Auditions Help Orchestras to Eliminate
   Gender Bias," *The Guardian*, October 14, 2013, https://
   www.theguardian.com/women-in-leadership/2013/oct/14/
   blind-auditions-orchestras-gender-bias.

2. United States Bureau of Labor Statistics – Economic News Release, "Persons with a Disability: Labor Force Characteristics Summary," February 23, 2023, https://www.bls.gov/news.release/disabl.nr0.htm.

3. Pavithra Mohan, "The Employment Rate for Disabled Workers Is Higher Than It Has Been in Years," *Fast Company*, October 14, 2022, https://www.fastcompany.com/90795083/the-employment-rate-for-disabled-workers-is-higher-than-it-has-been-in-years.

4. "At Hands In, a New Virtual World Shows the Future of Remote Work," *Virbela* (blog), March 20, 2022, https://www.virbela.com/blog/at-hands-in-a-new-virtual-world-shows-the-future-of-remote-work.

5. "DEI in XR: How to Facilitate Diverse Achievements," *Virbela* (blog), July 1, 2022, https://www.virbela.com/blog/dei-in-xr-how-to-facilitate-diverse-achievements.

6. Nadia Vatalidis, "How to Support Neurodivergence in the Workplace with Remote and Async Work," *Remote* (blog), accessed July 7, 2023, https://remote.com/blog/support-neurodivergence-workplace-remote-async.

7. "DEI in XR."

8. Karen R. Baker, "Designing an Inclusive Metaverse," *Harvard Business Review*, September 22, 2022, https://hbr.org/2022/09/designing-an-inclusive-metaverse?ab=at_art_art_1x4_s04.

Chapter 8: The Globalized Experience

1. Jack Kelly, "Upwork Study Says 19 Million Americans Plan on Relocating Due to Remote Work—Is This Likely Now That Omicron Subsided?" *Forbes*, June 15, 2022, https://www.forbes.com/sites/jackkelly/2022/03/14/upwork-study-says-19-million-americans-plan-on-relocating-due-to-remote-work-is-this-likely-now-that-omicron-subsided/?sh=45abcb0e1e7c.

2. Dwivedi et al., "Metaverse beyond the Hype."

3. Anuragini Shirish, Imed Boughzala, and Shirish C. Srivastava, "Bridging Cultural Discontinuities in Global Virtual Teams: Role of Cultural Intelligence," presented at the thirty-sixth International Conference on Information Systems in Fort Worth, Texas, USA (2015), accessed July 8, 2023. https://core.ac.uk/download/pdf/301367358.pdf.

4. Charlene Solomon, "Trends in Global Virtual Teams," Culture Wizard Virtual Teams Survey Report 2016, accessed July 8, 2023, http://cdn.culturewizard.com/PDF/Trends_in_VT_Report_4-17-2016.pdf?ref=hackernoon.com.

5. Charlene Solomon, "Trends in Global Virtual Teams."

6. Linn Van Dyne et al., "Sub-Dimensions of the Four Factor Model of Cultural Intelligence: Expanding the Conceptualization and Measurement of Cultural Intelligence," *Social and Personality Psychology Compass* 6, no. 4 (April 2012), 295–313. https://doi.org/10.1111/j.1751-9004.2012.00429.x.

7. PricewaterhouseCoopers, "PwC 2022 US Metaverse Survey," n.d., accessed July 8, 2023. https://www.pwc.com/us/en/tech-effect/emerging-tech/metaverse-survey.html.

8. PricewaterhouseCoopers, "Beyond the Hype: What Businesses Can Really Expect from the Metaverse in 2023," n.d., accessed July 8, 2023, https://www.pwc.com/us/en/tech-effect/innovation/metaverse-predictions.html?utm_leadsource=dynamicsignal&userid=227756&userchannelid=17235&channeltype=LinkedIn&postid=898a9e31-2e48-4aa0-81f8-3ced0b2a75af.

9. Charlie Fletcher, "Remote Work and the Digital Divide: How Your Business Can Overcome a New Inequality," Thrive Global, June 9, 2021, https://community.thriveglobal.com/remote-work-and-the-digital-divide-how-your-business-can-overcome-a-new-inequality/.

10. Kieron Allen, "Why the Metaverse May Create a Digital Divide," Acceleration Economy, October 17, 2022, https://accelerationeconomy.com/metaverse/why-the-metaverse-may-create-a-digital-divide/.

11. Fletcher, "Remote Work and the Digital Divide."

Chapter 9: Beyond "Building" Culture

1. Jim Harter, "Is Quiet Quitting Real?" Workplace – Gallup.com, last updated May 17, 2023, https://www.gallup.com/workplace/398306/quiet-quitting-real.aspx.

2. "6 Features Your Team Needs to Succeed in the Metaverse," *Virbela* (blog), July 22, 2022, https://www.virbela.com/blog/ 6-features-your-team-needs-to-succeed-in-the-metaverse.

3. David M. Levitt, "JLL's Peter Miscovich Wrote It Down: Flex Workplaces Are the Future," Commercial Observer, June 7, 2022, https://commercialobserver.com/2022/06/ peter-miscovich-office-design-flex/.

Chapter 10: Real-Life Connection in a Virtual World

1. Mark Purdy, "How the Metaverse Could Change Work," *Harvard Business Review*, April 5, 2022, https://hbr.org/2022/ 04/how-the-metaverse-could-change-work.

2. Zara Stone, "Will We Still Want a Metaverse When the Pandemic Is Over?" *Fast Company*, April 4, 2022, https://www. fastcompany.com/90737140/will-we-still-want-a-metaverse-when-the-pandemic-is-over?partner=rss&utm_source=rss&utm_ medium=feed&utm_campaign=rss+fastcompany&utm_ content=rss.

Chapter 11: A New Type of Education

1. Andrew Cohen, "NBA Introduces 'Metaverse Coach' at Tech Summit as Adam Silver Details Future Fan Experiences," *Sports Business Journal*, February 22, 2022, https://www. sportsbusinessjournal.com/Daily/Issues/2022/02/22/Technology/ nba-introduces-metaverse-coach-at-tech-summit-as-adam-silver-details-future-fanexperiences.

2. Adam Hadhazy, "Stanford Course Allows Students to Learn about Virtual Reality While Fully Immersed in VR Environments," Stanford News – Stanford University Communications, November 5, 2021, https://news.stanford.edu/2021/11/05/new-class-among-first-taught-entirely-virtual-reality/.

3. Hadhazy, "Stanford Course Allows Students."

4. Nir Kshetri, "5 Challenges of Taking College Classes in the Metaverse," *Fast Company*, September 19, 2022, https://www.fastcompany.com/90790011/5-challenges-of-taking-college-classes-in-the-metaverse?partner=rss&utm_source=rss&utm_medium=feed&utm_campaign=rss+fastcompany&utm_content=rss.

5. "About Virbela," Virbela, accessed August 25, 2023, https://www.virbela.com/company/about-virbela.

6. Purdy, "How the Metaverse Could Change Work."

7. Purdy, "How the Metaverse Could Change Work."

8. Purdy, "How the Metaverse Could Change Work."

9. Warehouse DT, "Amazon Robotics Builds Digital Twins of Warehouses with NVIDIA Omniverse and Isaac Sim," NVIDIA, March 23, 2022, video, 2:44, https://www.youtube.com/watch?v=-VQLqs6s9y0.

Chapter 12: Embracing Environmental Sustainability

1. Jessica Colarossi, "No, It's Not Your Imagination, the Air in Boston Is Cleaner," *The Brink*, Boston University Center for Information & Systems Engineering, April 16, 2020, https://www.bu.edu/articles/2020/no-its-not-your-imagination-the-air-in-boston-is-cleaner/.

2. Colarossi, "No, It's Not Your Imagination."

3. Ganga Shreedhar, Kate Laffan, and Laura M. Giurge, "Is Remote Work Actually Better for the Environment?" *Harvard Business Review*, March 7, 2022, https://hbr.org/2022/03/is-remote-work-actually-better-for-the-environment.

4. Adi Gaskell, "How Eco-Friendly Is Remote Working?" *Forbes*, October 21, 2021, https://www.forbes.com/sites/adigaskell/2021/10/21/how-eco-friendly-is-remote-working/?sh=3648681a1864.

5. Alba Badia et al., "A Take-Home Message from COVID-19 on Urban Air Pollution Reduction through Mobility Limitations and Teleworking," *Urban Sustainability* 1, no. 35 (August 17, 2021). https://www.nature.com/articles/s42949-021-00037-7.

6. David Fowler et al., "A Chronology of Global Air Quality," *Philosophical Transactions of the Royal Society A* 378, no. 2183 (September 28, 2020), https://royalsocietypublishing.org/doi/10.1098/rsta.2019.0314.

7. Deborah Cloutier, Brad A. Molotsky, Annette Michelle Willis, "ESG at a Tipping Point For Real Estate: Background, Recent Developments, and ESG Trends and Opportunities," RE Tech Advisors, November 2022, https://www.retechadvisors.com/esg-at-a-tipping-point-for-real-estate-background-recent-developments-and-esg-trends-and-opportunities/.

8. Joohee Cho and Hakyung Kate Lee, "South Korean Companies Move to Greener and Affordable Metaverse Office Spaces," ABC News, July 31, 2022, https://abcnews.go.com/International/south-korean-companies-move-greener-affordable-metaverse-office/story?id=87624178.

9. Veronica Poole and Kristen Sullivan, "Tectonic Shifts: How ESG Is Changing Business, Moving Markets, and Driving Regulation," Deloitte Insights, October 29, 2021, https://www2.deloitte.com/us/en/insights/topics/strategy/esg-disclosure-regulation.html.

10. PricewaterhouseCoopers, "Environmental, Social and Governance (ESG)," n.d., accessed July 8, 2023, https://www.pwc.com/gx/en/issues/esg.html.

11. Gaskell, "How Eco-Friendly Is Remote Working?"

12. FULL Creative, "The Incredible Shrinking Office," n.d., accessed July 8, 2023, https://full.io/incredible-shrinking-office.

13. Stephen Nellis, "Salesforce Acts on Climate, Requiring Suppliers to Set Carbon Goals," Reuters, April 29, 2021, https://www.reuters.com/business/sustainable-business/salesforce-acts-climate-requiring-suppliers-set-carbon-goals-2021-04-29/.

14. Eric Friedrichsen, "Business Travel Won't Be More Sustainable Post-COVID Unless Companies Take Action," World Economic Forum, September 1, 2021, https://www.weforum.org/agenda/2021/09/business-travel-wont-be-more-sustainable-post-covid-unless-companies-take-action/.

15. Steve Lohr, "The Internet Eats Up Less Energy Than You Might Think," *New York Times*, June 24, 2021, https://www.nytimes.com/2021/06/24/technology/computer-energy-use-study.html.

16. Lohr, "The Internet Eats Up Less Energy."

17. Shreedhar, Laffan, and Giurge, "Is Remote Work Actually Better for the Environment?"

18. Shreedhar, Laffan, and Giurge, "Is Remote Work Actually Better for the Environment?"

19. National Museum of American History Behring Center, "Green Business," Smithsonian: National Museum of American History, accessed July 8, 2023, https://americanhistory.si.edu/american-enterprise-exhibition/global-era/green-business.

INDEX

O

O'Carroll, Shay, 166
Oculus, 77
OMNUS, 15
OMNUS Metaverse campus
    (Omnusverse), 1
    fluidity between virtual and real
        worlds, 2–3
    Information Desk, 2
    island amenities, 2
    main auditorium, 1–2
    wardrobe room, 103
online disinhibition, 76
open-door policy, 107–9
optical bias, 102–5
organizational benefits of
    Metaverse, 119–20

P

pivoting
    adapting to survive, 24
    COVID-19 pandemic and, 15–17
    evaluating purpose and
        resources, 21–22
    eXp Realty, 7–15, 17–19
    Hewlett Packard Enterprise, 20–21
    importance of adaptability, 24
    innovation and, 22–23
    to lead, 15–17
    Netflix, 23
    service-sector organizations, 19–22
PixelMax, 152, 165–66
praise and commendation, 81
privacy and safety
    accountability, 75
    biometric tracking,
        55–58, 64, 67–68
    digital pioneers, 68
    guardians, 65–66
    hardware, 63–64
    importance of, 69
    individual, 60–61
    information, 61–62
    medical workspaces, 61

Metaverse as safe space, 117
monitoring and data
    tracking, 57–60
self-governance, 66–68
social media, 59
software, 62–63
"virtual hedge," 64–65
productivity, 85–98
    avatars and, 93–97
    Joint Strike Fighter (JSF) pro-
        gram, 95–96
    purpose drives output, 85–89
    quiet quitting, 89–93
    relationship between entertainment
        and, 148–49, 154–55
    virtual workspace vs. traditional
        workspace, 93–95
professional isolation, 132–33
profitability. *See also* pivoting
    environmental sustainabil-
        ity and, 178
    eXp Realty, 13
    long-term view of, 19
    privacy and safety and, 68
    shedding cost of physical real
        estate, 25
Publix, 40
Purdy, Mark, 165
PwC, 62, 63, 108, 127

Q

quiet quitting, 89–93

R

real-life connections, 141–58
    "be well" strategies, 151–55
    hybrid Metaverse wedding, 142–44
    sense of community,
        146–51, 155–57
    shift in socialization experi-
        ences, 144–46
real-time location tracking, 57–58
Recology, 40–41

ABOUT THE AUTHOR

Image courtesy of Virbela

JASON GESING, a pioneer in Metaverse-based work environments since 2010 and an attorney, is the co-founder and CEO of OMNUS Technologies, Inc. and OMNUS Law, LLP. OMNUS companies are dedicated to transforming and improving the lives of attorneys and other service professionals by using technology to reduce costs and unlock dominant competitive advantages. Prior to OMNUS, Jason served as the CEO of eXp Realty (2016–2018 and 2019–2023), a Metaverse-based real estate brokerage and, at the end of 2022, the largest independent real estate company in the world. Jason helped lead and drive the growth of eXp Realty from fewer than fifty agents in early 2010 to more than 86,000 agents and brokers across twenty-four countries by the end of 2022. He is committed to fostering civility, equal opportunity, and access to justice. Jason actively supports individuals and organizations dedicated to combating disinformation in the digital age.